ideas for great

HOME LIGHTING

By Scott Atkinson
and the Editors of Sunset Books

Sunset Books ■ Menlo Park, California

Sunset Books

vice president, general manager:
Richard A. Smeby

vice president, editorial director:
Bob Doyle

production director:
Lory Day

director of operations:
Rosann Sutherland

sales development director:
Linda Barker

art director:
Vasken Guiragossian

Staff for this book:

developmental editor:
Linda J. Selden

copy editor:
Phyllis Elving

photo director/stylist:
JoAnn Masaoka Van Atta

page layout:
Kathy Avanzino Barone

illustrations:
Beverley Bozarth Colgan

principal photographer:
Philip Harvey

production coordinator:
Eligio Hernandez

proofreader:
Mary Roybal

*Cover: Three low-voltage pendants complete a modern, multilayered
lighting scheme. For details, see page 54. Architect: Backen, Arragoni
& Ross. Cover design by Vasken Guiragossian. Photography by Philip
Harvey. Photo direction by JoAnn Masaoka Van Atta.*

In the spotlight

Indoors and out, today's home designs are enhanced
by fresh lighting schemes to match. This new addition
to Sunset's popular "Ideas for Great…" series shines
a bright light on the latest looks in home lighting. If
you're browsing for techniques, inspiration, or shopping tips, you've come to the right place.

Many professionals, manufacturers, and homeown-
ers shared their expertise with us or allowed us to pho-
tograph in their homes. We'd especially like to thank
J. Art Hatley of Fiberstars, Inc. of Fremont, California;
Leslie Siegel of Cherish Gaines Lighting Systems of
Berkeley, California; Doug Ascher of Universal Light
Source of San Francisco, California; LIMN of San
Francisco, California; Stanford Electric Works of Palo
Alto, California; Coast Lighting of Redwood City,
California; and The Home Depot of East Palo Alto,
California.

Credits for lighting designs featured in specific
photos are listed on pages 126–127.

contents

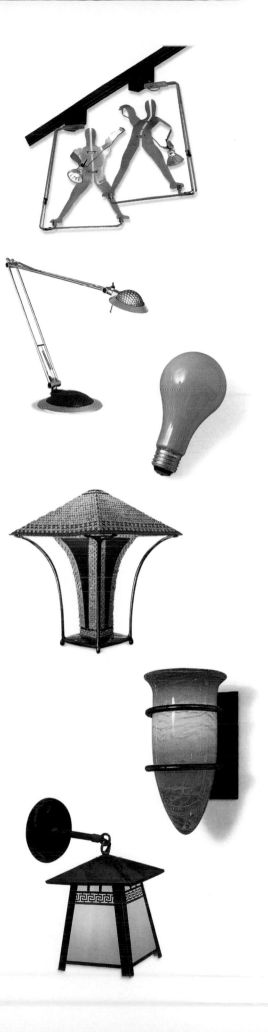

paint it with light

FLEXIBLE, EFFICIENT, and a little bit fun—that's the plan for today's home lighting. Take your pick: crisp highlights or moody shadows; bold strokes or a soft, flattering wash. Or mix them together. Indoors or out, you'll discover lighting products and techniques that deliver comfort, safety, and style.

Flexibility is the new byword; glare is the big bad wolf in lighting lingo. Flexibility means multiple light sources or *layers* operated by multiple controls, allowing you to dial in your mood; dimmer switches provide fine-tuning options. Motion sensors, timers, and daylight sensors abound. Computerized control panels are gaining steam.

Light sources are more energy-efficient and more adaptable than ever before. Fluorescent bulbs and tubes are much improved—just in time, given energy codes requiring ambient fluorescent light in some locales. Once available only in "cool-white" (read "ghoulish blue-green"), fluorescents now come in about 200 colors; fixture choices are expanding, too, with the advent of compact fluorescent bulbs. Long-lasting halogen bulbs are another option, delivering punch and focus. Also up-and-coming are decorative fiber optics, cold cathode, and an "industrial" source: metal halide.

Fixtures are shrinking in size. In today's lighting philosophy, unless you want to feature it, it should be invisible. What if you *do* want to feature your fixtures? You'll find endless new designs, from halogen pendants and contemporary wall sconces to tiny, jazzy low-voltage tracks and rope lights.

Outdoors, good lighting provides safety and security, but lighting pros also speak of increased curb value and the way exterior lighting expands interior space. Today's outdoor lighting designs are subtle, even those incorporating sophisticated security options. Like indoor schemes, new outdoor installations tend to be multilayered and flexible.

Ready to light it up? This book takes a three-phase approach. The first section, "A Planning Primer," paints the basic terms and techniques you'll need to know. Next, "Great Lighting Ideas" makes a colorful, room-by-room house tour—and then heads outdoors. Want to shop? Turn to "A Shopper's Guide" for the scoop on bulbs, fixtures, and controls.

A PLANNING PRIMER

THE PLEASURES of good lighting have an elusive quality. When you walk into a room with a successful lighting design, you don't remark "What fantastic lighting!" But your eyes sense that everything is comfortably visible, and you feel somehow both stimulated and at ease. In fact, our eyes don't observe the light itself, but rather the things on which it shines; a great lighting scheme serves as a silent partner in enhancing the surroundings. THIS CHAPTER GIVES YOU a good start toward bringing this partner into your home. In these pages we identify the properties of effective lighting and explain them in clear terms to help you achieve the best lighting design for your own situation. FOR INSPIRATION AND IDEAS to use both indoors and out, browse through "Great Lighting Ideas," beginning on page 27. And for guidance in choosing bulbs, fixtures, and innovative controls, see "A Shopper's Guide," pages 93–125.

designing with light

HOME LIGHTING *is the art of painting light and shadow onto a dark canvas. The best lighting designer is a problem solver, determining where light is needed and then directing it there with economy and flair. Professionals approach lighting with the following arsenal of terms and tools; you can, too.*

Four types of light

Lighting designers have traditionally split lighting into three basic categories: task, accent, and ambient. But as a counterpoint to the current trend of making basic fixtures unobtrusive, a fourth type is emerging: decorative light, using fixtures that are deliberately featured. Here are definitions of all four categories.

TASK LIGHTING. This bright light illuminates a particular area where a visual activity takes place—reading, sewing, or preparing food, for example. Task lighting is often achieved by means of individual fixtures that direct a tight pattern of light onto the work surface.

Adjustability is important for task lighting. So is shielding—hiding the bulb from direct sight. It's best to aim task lighting at an angle so it won't cause "hot spots" or throw shadows onto the work area. Where possible, two sources are better than one.

ACCENT LIGHTING. Similar to task lighting in that it consists largely of directional light, accent lighting is used to focus attention on artwork, to highlight architectural features, to set a mood, or to provide a sense of drama.

Beam spread, intensity, and color are often critical considerations for accent light. Low-voltage halogen bulbs (pages 98–99) produce especially clean white accent light, and they are available in a wide variety of intensities and beam patterns.

AMBIENT LIGHTING. With ambient lighting, the undefined areas of a room are filled with a soft level of general light—say, enough for someone to watch television by or to navigate safely through the room. An ambient glow not only makes a room more inviting, it helps

TASK LIGHTING

DECORATIVE LIGHTING

AMBIENT LIGHTING

people look their best, filling in harsh shadows created by stronger point sources.

Ambient lighting usually comes from indirect fixtures that provide diffuse illumination. Directional fixtures aimed at a wall can also produce a wash of soft light. Or consider built-in lighting coves, cornices, valances, and soffits. These simple architectural devices ensure that light sources are shielded from view, allowing light to spill out around the shields.

DECORATIVE LIGHTING. These fixtures draw attention to themselves as objects. The classic chandelier is an example; newer options include zoomy low-voltage pendant fixtures, neon, and fiber optics. Decorative strip lights (pages 110–111) can add sparkle and warmth to a room while highlighting architectural lines. And don't forget candles, either the traditional kind or electric ones.

ACCENT LIGHTING

This multiuse dining space has flexible, multilayered light sources to match. Discreet downlights shine down on dining table, artwork, and collectibles. Striking wall sconces add decorative style and ambient fill light.

The art of layering

One basic rule of efficient lighting is to put light where you need it. But to ensure an attractive, comfortable lighting scheme, you must also think about balancing light—that is, creating an effective spread of dim and strong light throughout a room. A laundry room, hallway, or guest bedroom may not need more than one set of fixtures, but multiple-use areas such as living rooms, great rooms, and kitchens present more of a challenge.

The key to balancing light is layering. That's where the four different lighting types come in.

Lighting designers first identify the main activity areas, or the room's focal point or points (having two or three is often best). This is where they direct the brightest layer of light. Next, a middle layer provides interest in specific areas without detracting from the focal points. The last layer fills in the background.

The first two layers are supplied by task or accent lighting, depending on what is being lit. The lower-level "fill" or ambient light is usually indirect (like that provided by wall sconces, for example). The ratio of the brightest light in the room to the fill light usually should be about 3

Getting control

Dimmers and control panels (see pages 118–119) can help you custom-tailor light for multiple uses and decorative effects. Dimmers—also called rheostats—enable you to set a fixture or group of fixtures at any brightness level, from soft glow to full throttle. They're also energy savers. Be aware, though, that some light sources—notably fluorescents—can be difficult or unduly expensive to dim; bone up on your options when you go shopping.

Control panels allow you to monitor a number of functions or "scenes" from one spot. Originally designed for commercial use, they're now showing up in residential lighting, too. And as the world of computers meets that of residential design, software-programmed lighting and/or "smart house" systems have become a reality. These allow an almost infinite degree of lighting control and flexibility—for a price.

Beware of glare

One of the most important considerations in the placement of light fixtures is the glare they produce. Direct glare—as from a bare light bulb—is the worst kind. Deeply recessed fixtures or fixtures with black baffles or small apertures (see page 115) can remedy the problem. Clip-on louvers and shutters also cut glare. Silvered-bowl bulbs (page 95) help tame the glare from traditional lamps and fixtures, as do diffusing shades or covers.

Also watch out for reflected glare—light bouncing off an object into your eyes. Light reflects off an object at the same angle as it strikes it (as shown at right); if the angle is too steep, the light produces a hot spot. The safety range is about 30 to 45 degrees from vertical.

A fixture located directly over a flat, shiny surface—a dining room table, for instance—can create "veiling" glare. Objects placed on the table can help deflect this glare; a dimmer can also reduce the reflected light to a comfortable level.

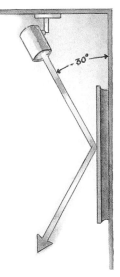

To minimize reflected glare, light artwork from a 30- to 45-degree angle.

to 1—at most 5 to 1. Ratios of 10 or even 100 to 1 are great for high drama but uncomfortable for everyday living. To learn how to check light ratios, read "Testing Your Ideas" on page 17.

Once the essential layers are in place, you can add decorative fixtures, if you like. General light will appear to emanate from these sources, but since you've already set up levels of task, accent, and ambient layers, this light isn't necessary in the overall scheme. When chandeliers are used as primary light givers, they can produce harsh glare; dimmed to a comfortable glow, they become inviting decorative additions.

Tricks of the trade

You can use light both to draw the eye to the architectural features and decor in your house and to help disguise any aspects you'd like to play down. Designers mix and match the basic lighting tricks shown below. In addition, consider the following time-tested techniques.

■ CEILINGS can pose problems, or they can become special features. If your ceilings seem too low, bounced light from uplights can visually "raise" them. Cathedral or beamed ceilings can take on new importance with uplighting. Many designers also use beams to hold track lighting (see pages 112–113), taking advantage of architectural lines to disguise the track.

A common problem in older homes is rough or patchy plaster. For dealing with this and also with ceilings that seem too high, the solution is the same: keep light off the ceiling by using downlighting. The darker surface will seem lower, and imperfections will go unnoticed.

■ ROOM DIMENSIONS can be altered visually with lighting tricks. Small rooms can look open and airy with the right lighting, and large rooms can be made to appear cozy and inviting.

Washing the walls of a small room with an even layer of light seems to push them outward, expanding the perceived sense of space. When the wall is a light color, the effect is even more pronounced.

Illuminating a large room with a few soft pools of light concentrated on important objects or areas makes it seem smaller and more intimate; the lighted areas absorb more attention than the room as a whole.

Narrow rooms benefit from lighting trickery, too. Placing lights along shorter walls draws the eye away from the long ones, resulting in a "wider" space.

■ WINDOWS, sources of daylight, can seem like dark mirrors or black holes if left uncovered at night. One way to avoid reflections is to light

◄ DOWNLIGHTING

This look is probably familiar—after all, sunlight is downlighting. The degree of focus determines the effect. The tighter the beam, the more drama and the heavier the shadows.

SILHOUETTING ►

Like backlighting (above right), the light here comes from behind—but in this case it faces the background, dropping the cube into dark relief. In daylight, cube and background are similar colors; it's the lighting that makes one appear bright and the other near-black.

UPLIGHTING ►

The opposite of downlighting (above left), this technique makes objects seem to "float" from below. Uplighting can create strong light contrasts; for a softer look, add fill light from above.

the area outside a window or patio door to a high enough level that lights inside balance those outside. Another solution is to use opaque pendant fixtures or recessed downlights, so that only the lighted areas reflect, not the light sources themselves.

■ **MASONRY SURFACES** such as brick walls or a stone fireplace take on new beauty when lighted at an acute angle, a technique called "grazing." You can play up the textures of fabric walls and window coverings in a similar way.

■ **ARTWORK** can be lit in a variety of ways. For the most dramatic effect, spotlight works of art from above or below: a 30-degree angle off the vertical is best—even less if you wish to play up the surface texture of a particular piece.

Frame-mounted picture lights are also available (see pages 106–107), though these may not illuminate a large painting evenly.

Sculpture and other three-dimensional objects usually call for lighting from two sides to minimize shadows. Or you can emphasize shadows or a silhouette by aiming a single spot from behind or below. Don't hesitate to experiment with uplighting, downlighting, grazing, or backlighting.

■ **INDOOR PLANTS** need light to help them look their best—and to help them grow. Try silhouetting plants with concealed uplights or backlighting them against a luminous screen or lighted wall. Or bounce light down through the foliage with a fixture recessed in the ceiling or suspended from it.

■ **COLLECTIONS** can be lit evenly overall, or spotlights can be focused on individual pieces. Downlighting shelves or display cabinets may make upper shelves cast shadows on shelves below. Backlighting, lighting vertically from the sides, or attaching lights under the front edges of shelves will eliminate this problem. Concealing fixtures will help keep down glare and lend a clean look to your display.

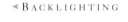

◄ BACKLIGHTING

The light comes from behind, aimed toward the object. Backlighting makes translucent objects—like this glass vase— glow with light. Note the "rim-lighting" effect where light rays bend around the vase's outline.

◄ BOUNCE LIGHTING

Also called indirect lighting, this is the softest light form, often used for ambient fill. Light hits a wall or ceiling, then bounces back to the subject. Compare this to downlighting on the facing page: it's the same ball, but here highlights and shadows are much softer.

GRAZING ►

Use this technique to emphasize textures— such as masonry, fabric, a plastered wall—or even an oil painting. Place the light source near the surface and "skim" light across it. If the light spread is broader and a little less steep, it's called "wall washing."

color and reflectance

BEFORE CHOOSING *light sources for a room, it helps to know some basic theory about the nature of light and color. The interaction between a light source and a room's colors and surfaces creates two additional subjects to consider: color rendition and reflectance.*

What is light?

What our retinas perceive as "light" is just part of a wider range of electromagnetic radiation produced in the form of waves. The intensity of light waves creates their color. Infrared rays, ultraviolet rays, X-rays, radio waves, and heat are part of the spectrum that we can't see.

We think of midday sunlight as the standard for pure white light color. When daylight is passed through a prism, however, it is actually rendered as equal parts of a continuous spectrum including red, orange, yellow, green, blue, and violet (see the drawing below).

In contrast, artificial light sources give off varying amounts of color. Incandescent light includes most of the spectrum but has a large proportion of yellow and red. When dimmed, incandescent light becomes even redder.

Many people think of fluorescent light as being low in red and high in green and blue light waves, but in fact fluorescent tubes now come in more than 200 colors. Quartz halogen produces brighter, "whiter" light than either incandescent or fluorescent sources; it's popular for commercial display and museum lighting as well as for residential accenting.

THE COLOR SPECTRUM

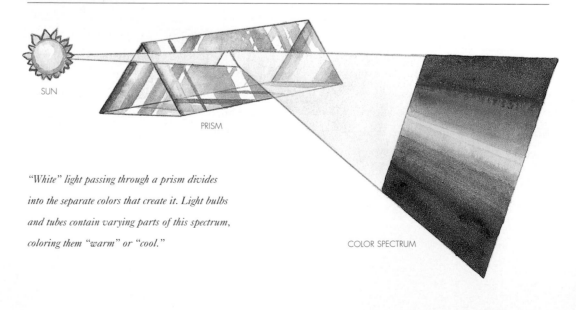

SUN

PRISM

COLOR SPECTRUM

"White" light passing through a prism divides into the separate colors that create it. Light bulbs and tubes contain varying parts of this spectrum, coloring them "warm" or "cool."

Light bulbs are formally rated by color temperature, measured in degrees Kelvin (K). Temperatures below 3,500°K are warm-toned; higher temperatures are increasingly blue, or cool. The chart at right shows the position of several standard light sources on such a "thermometer."

Color rendition

How we perceive the color of an object is determined by two things: the surface color of the object itself and the color in the light that shines on it. The color of a blue vase under a blue light will be heightened, because the color of the light intensifies the blue of the vase. Under a red light, the same blue vase will appear dull and grayish, because the red light waves are absorbed and there are no blue waves to be reflected by the vase.

Because lighting can affect the apparent color of fabrics and wallpaper, it's always a good idea to choose furnishings and decorating materials under the same type of light you'll be using at home. If possible, bring home a swatch of material or a paint sample, or take sample materials to a lighting store. Today's "light labs"— showrooms where you can directly compare light sources—make this evaluation a lot easier.

Reflectance

The colors and textures of a room's walls, ceiling, and floor not only affect the room's decor but also contribute to the general light level according to their reflectance—that is, the degree to which they reflect light. Colors and textures of furnishings and display objects can affect overall light levels, too.

Colors that contain a lot of white reflect a large amount of light, of course, while darker colors absorb more light. A white object reflects 80 percent of the light that strikes it, while a black object reflects 5 percent or less. The illumination in a room with light-colored walls is distributed farther and more evenly as it is reflected from surface to surface until it gradually

A COLOR THERMOMETER

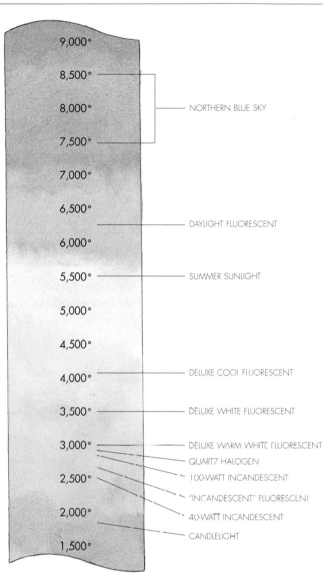

9,000°	
8,500°	— NORTHERN BLUE SKY
8,000°	
7,500°	
7,000°	
6,500°	— DAYLIGHT FLUORESCENT
6,000°	
5,500°	— SUMMER SUNLIGHT
5,000°	
4,500°	
4,000°	— DELUXE COOL FLUORESCENT
3,500°	— DELUXE WHITE FLUORESCENT
3,000°	— DELUXE WARM WHITE FLUORESCENT
	— QUARTZ HALOGEN
	— 100-WATT INCANDESCENT
2,500°	— "INCANDESCENT" FLUORESCENT
	— 40-WATT INCANDESCENT
2,000°	
	— CANDLELIGHT
1,500°	

diminishes. For this reason, if you were to redecorate your living room by covering creamy white walls with a rich blue wallpaper, you'd find that you needed more light sources and bulbs of higher wattage to reach the same light levels as before.

Texture plays a part in reflectance, too. Matte finishes diffuse light; glossy finishes bounce light onto other surfaces. Thus, a room with fabric-covered walls requires more fixtures or brighter bulbs than a room with painted walls in order to achieve the same level of light.

how much is enough?

LIGHT LEVELS *are partly a matter of individual preference. Some people grow accustomed to brightly lit offices and want similar uniform illumination in their homes. Others feel more relaxed and secure with relatively low light levels, preferring to focus on the area where they're reading, working, or dining. The current thinking is toward bright, efficient lighting in task areas, with surroundings more softly lit.*

Taking stock

So how much task light is "enough?" When planning, consider these factors:

- How difficult is the task to be performed?
- How much speed and accuracy does the task require?
- How much color contrast is there among materials involved in the task?
- How good is the eyesight of the person who will be engaged in the activity?

If an older person will be doing embroidery on a dark cloth with richly colored thread, lots of light will probably be required; the task calls for a high degree of accuracy, and the weak contrast between the fabric and the thread is hard on older eyes. For less demanding visual activities, such as reading the newspaper or watching television, light levels can be much lower.

Measuring lumens

One method for measuring and planning light levels involves adding up the amount of light—measured in lumens—emitted by all the bulbs in a certain area. If you look at the sleeve around a light bulb, you'll see that it states both the bulb's wattage (the amount of electricity used by the bulb) and the number of lumens (amount of light) that the bulb produces. Lumen outputs vary from one manufacturer to another, and they diminish as bulbs age.

As a rule of thumb, the most difficult visual tasks, such as embroidery, require a total of at least 2,500 lumens in an average-size room, with the greatest number of lumens concentrated at the work location. A casual task, such as watching television, requires from 1,500 to 2,000 lumens. To figure total lumens, just add up the lumen outputs of all the bulbs in the room.

For reference purposes, a standard 40-watt incandescent A-bulb (the familiar pear shape) puts out about 455 lumens, a 75-watt bulb casts 1,190 lumens, and a 150-watt bulb produces 2,880 lumens.

Measuring footcandles

A second and more precise method of measuring light levels uses the footcandle, the amount of illumination provided by a single lumen distributed over a foot-square surface.

Lighting designers and engineers have determined standard footcandle levels needed to perform ordinary household tasks. The chart below includes both a high and a low number of footcandles; the higher level is recommended for older people, the lower level for younger eyes. While these are recommended levels, individuals may prefer more or less light. Remember that dimmers (page 118) allow you to dial light up for one use, and down for another.

Experts measure footcandles with a special footcandle meter, but you can use the light meter built into a 35mm camera; for directions, see "Testing Your Ideas" at right.

Providing enough light for task areas is of primary importance, but care should also be taken to provide the surrounding areas with ambient light. In rooms with task lighting, the recommended ambient light level is 20 footcandles or about a third of the task area's footcandle value, whichever is less. For rooms where the main activity is entertaining or relaxing, a level of 5 to 10 footcandles is recommended. Entries, stairs, and passageways should also have a general light level of 5 to 10 footcandles.

RECOMMENDED MINIMUM FOOTCANDLES

Activity	Footcandles
Entertaining	10–20
Dining	10–20
Casual reading	20–50
Grooming	20–50
Kitchen, laundry—general light	20–50
Kitchen—food preparation	50–100
Prolonged reading or studying	50–100
Workshop activities	50–100
Sewing, medium-colored fabrics	50–100
Sewing, dark fabrics	100–200
Hobbies involving fine detail	100–200

TESTING YOUR IDEAS

It pays to know what kind of light you want and where it should be placed before you invest in fixtures for a room. But how can you find out? For basic experimenting you won't need much: a standard utility lamp or trouble light, a 1- or 2-pound coffee can, a homemade paper shade, a few bulbs, perhaps a table lamp borrowed from another room, and one or more extension cords. You'll also need a stepladder if you're planning to test ceiling fixtures. The coffee can, with its bottom cut out, gives you a kind of directional spotlight; the utility lamp's reflector produces a broader-beamed, more general light; and a paper shade casts a soft, diffuse glow.

Experts use a special meter to measure footcandles, but you can use the light meter built into a 35mm camera that has manually adjustable settings. To determine the number of footcandles of light reaching your kitchen counter, for example, prop a large sheet of white paper or cardboard on the counter at a 45-degree angle. Set the camera's ASA dial at 100 and the shutter speed at $\frac{1}{15}$ of a second. The f-stop reading you get can then be translated into the approximate footcandle level, as listed below.

At ASA 100 and $\frac{1}{15}$ second:

f4 = 10 footcandles
f5.6 = 20 footcandles
f8 = 40 footcandles
f11 = 80 footcandles
f16 = 160 footcandles
f19 (between f16 and f22) = 240 footcandles

The camera also lets you preview light ratios. From a central vantage point, aim the camera at both brightly lit objects and shadowy areas, then compare readings. A 3-to-1 light ratio equals a $\frac{1}{2}$ f-stop difference between the highest and lowest reading; a 4-to-1 ratio equals a difference of 2 f-stops, and a 10-to-1 ratio equals a difference of $3\frac{1}{2}$ f-stops.

choosing light sources

DO YOU WANT *warm light or cool light? Spotlights or broad beams? Discreet downlights or futuristic halogen pendants? You'd think fixtures would be the first thing to come up in any lighting discussion, but professional designers first pick the bulbs—which they call "lamps"—and only then the appropriate fixtures to shape the light and add style.*

Light bulbs and tubes

Bulbs and tubes can be grouped in general categories according to how they produce light. The following is a brief breakdown. Photos and charts in "A Shopper's Guide," starting on page 93, present the broad spectrum of available bulbs and tubes, with information about wattages, light outputs, efficiency, and color rendition.

INCANDESCENT BULBS. A tungsten filament burning inside a glass bulb filled with inert gas, usually argon, produces the warm incandescent light that we're all familiar with. The most common incandescent bulb is the pear-shaped A-bulb, but many other shapes and sizes are available (see pages 94–95).

Most incandescents are designed for standard 120-volt household current, but low-voltage versions (see page 21) are also available.

Incandescent bulbs have excellent color rendering properties but, in general, are not very efficient. While A-bulbs are inexpensive to buy, they don't last nearly as long as other bulb types. Use a more efficient source (such as fluorescent light) when the warmth and excel-

INCANDESCENT
BULB

lent color-rendering properties of incandescent light are not crucial.

FLUORESCENT TUBES. When electricity passes through a fluorescent tube, it burns the mercury vapor there, producing ultraviolet light that is reradiated as visible light by the phosphors coating the inside of the tube. Because the light comes evenly from the entire tube surface, it spreads in all directions, creating a steady, shadowless light. Tubes require a ballast to ignite and maintain the electrical flow. You can also get energy-saving compact fluorescents that screw into a socket; these can be used to replace incandescent bulbs in regular fixtures. For details, see pages 96–97.

Fluorescent tubes are unrivaled for energy efficiency, and they last far longer than incandescent bulbs. In some energy-conscious places, ambient lighting in kitchens and bathrooms *must* be fluorescent.

FLUORESCENT TUBE

Older fluorescent tubes have been criticized for noise, flicker, and poor color rendition. Electronic ballasts and better fixture shielding against glare have remedied the first two problems; as for color, manufacturers have developed fluorescents in a wide spectrum of hues, from very warm (about 2,700°K) to very cool (about 6,300°K).

HALOGEN BULBS. Containing a tiny quartz filament and a chemical coating (halogens), these bulbs produce a brighter beam and last longer than incandescent sources. They're excellent for task lighting, pinpoint accenting, and other dramatic effects. Many halogen fixtures use tube-shaped halogen bulbs, but there are a variety of shapes on the market (see pages 98–99), including bulbs shaped to replace common incandescent A-bulbs, and various reflectors. Halogen is usually low-voltage but may be standard 120-volt household current.

Halogen's one disadvantage, besides the initial

HALOGEN BULB

cost, is that it's very hot. To be used safely, halogen bulbs must be used in halogen fixtures. Shop carefully; some fixtures on the market are not UL-approved.

OTHER SOURCES. *High-intensity discharge (HID)* bulbs produce light when electricity excites specific gases in pressurized bulbs. Requiring special fixtures and ballasts, these lights may take several minutes to ignite after being switched on. The color emitted by most HID bulbs is rather unflattering, but they offer long life and efficiency. One HID source—mercury vapor—is commonly used for outdoor security lighting. For details, see page 103.

Neon light is also generated by electricity passing through a gas; neon gas glows orange-red, while other gases give off a variety of colors. Neon (page 100) is almost strictly decorative. *Cold cathode,* a close cousin of neon, puts out more light and is useful for ambient or indirect lighting as well as decoration. *Fiber optics* (pages 100–101) allow for exciting installations but at present are quite pricey.

HIGH-INTENSITY DISCHARGE BULB

ENERGY-SAVING OPTIONS

In the average household, lighting accounts for 15 to 20 percent of all electrical power consumed. By carefully planning new lighting or making a few changes in your present habits, you can trim your energy consumption and costs. Here's a checklist of 16 energy-saving tips to get you started:

- Switch off lights when you leave a room
- Paint your walls light colors
- Take advantage of daylight
- Emphasize task lighting
- Buy compact fluorescent bulbs
- Dust light bulbs regularly
- Buy three-way bulbs
- Use energy-saving night-lights

- Use the lowest-wattage light bulbs possible
- Move lamps toward the corners of rooms
- Add dimmers to your lamps and light circuits
- Install timer switches
- Opt for low-voltage garden lights
- Install motion detectors and photocells outdoors
- Make security lights fluorescent or mercury vapor
- Go solar to power garden lighting

a planning

TORCHÈRE

PENDANT

WALL
SCONCE

TASK LIGHT

Light fixtures

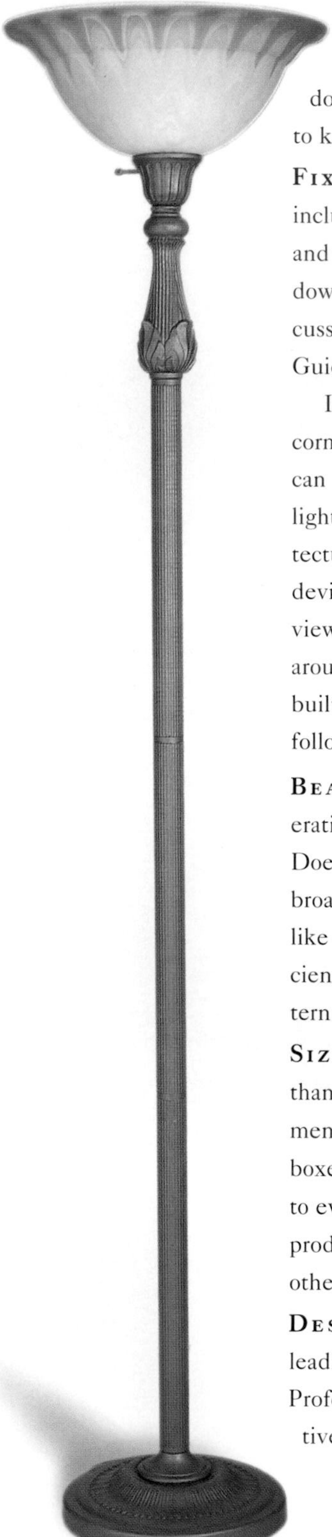

Once you've formed some ideas about the kinds of light sources you need, selecting fixtures would appear to be easy. But given the great variety available today, finding the right fixtures can be confusing and downright complicated. Here are some points to keep in mind.

FIXTURE TYPES. Your basic fixture options include movable lamps, surface-mounted ceiling and wall lights, track systems, and recessed downlights. Each of these is discussed in detail in "A Shopper's Guide," pages 104–115.

In addition, built-in coves, cornices, valances, and soffits can be used when indirect lighting is desired. Architectural in design, these devices shield light sources from view, allowing light to spill out around the shields. You'll find these built-in fixtures in action throughout the following section, "Great Lighting Ideas."

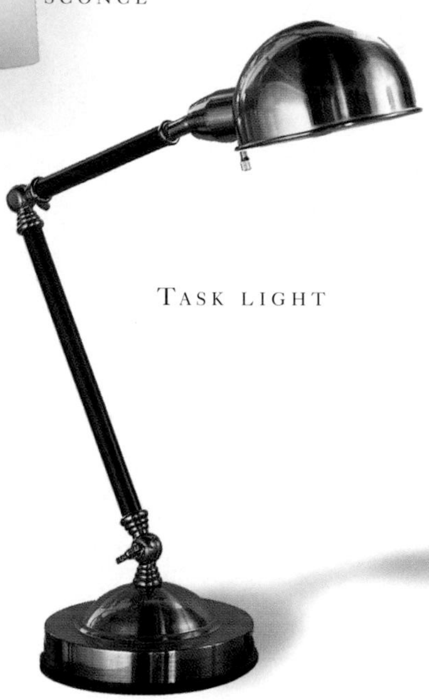

BEAM PATTERN. One of the primary considerations for any fixture is how it directs light. Does it create a narrow, focused beam of light, a broad, diffuse spread—or something in between, like the torchère shown at left? For greatest efficiency, match the fixture's light distribution pattern to the lighting need.

SIZE. Fixtures often seem smaller in the store than they will in your home. Take measurements of your top choices; then hold bowls or boxes of the same sizes in place back at home to evaluate the scale. Manufacturers often produce fixtures in graded sizes, so ask about other possibilities.

DESIGN. Personal taste will be your guide, leading you to whatever suits your decor. Professionals have found that a sense of decorative continuity can be created by using similar fixtures throughout a home. In response, manufacturers offer "families" of fixtures that include spotlights, pendants, track lights, and ceiling fixtures.

COST. When calculating costs, there's more to consider than the price of the fixture. The energy consumption of the bulbs or tubes that will be used in the fixture is a significant factor; for a comparative look at light bulbs, turn to pages 102–103. Also, be aware that some fixtures are more efficient than others, transmitting a higher percentage of the light produced by the bulbs or

BUILT-IN COVE LIGHTING

TRACK

RECESSED DOWNLIGHT

tubes they contain and, therefore, providing more light for the amount of electricity consumed.

FLEXIBILITY. Tastes, habits, and styles change over the years. Your lighting system should be flexible enough to accommodate such changes. Movable or adjustable lamps, of course, are flexible by design. But track systems and even recessed downlights can be changed, too. You can move fixtures along a track or readjust the way they're aimed. A regular built-in downlight can be transformed into an accent light or a wall-washing light.

MAINTENANCE. To operate efficiently, all fixtures need to be cleaned regularly. Kitchens, bathrooms, and work areas in particular demand fixtures that are easy to reach and clean. For hard-to-reach areas, such as above stairs, a fixture with a long-lived fluorescent or halogen bulb is a good choice.

WHAT ABOUT LOW-VOLTAGE?

Low-voltage lighting for indoor use has become common on the residential scene. Operating on 12 or 24 volts, low-voltage lights require transformers (sometimes built into the fixtures) to step down the voltage from standard 120-volt household circuits. The small bulbs are especially useful for accent lighting, where light must be baffled or precisely directed onto a small area. The compact fixtures that house the bulbs are decorative in their own right.

Low-voltage fixtures and bulbs are relatively expensive to buy, but this kind of lighting can be energy-efficient if carefully planned. To learn more about your options, see "A Shopper's Guide," beginning on page 93.

CABLE LIGHT

a planning primer

moving outdoors

PLAN OUTDOOR LIGHTING, *either low-voltage or 120-volt, much as you would indoor lighting. Begin by deciding where you'll need light at night for safety, activity, and security. Then you can add decorative or festive accents—though in many cases functional lighting can also be decorative.*

Less is best

Because the contrast between darkness and a light source is so great, glare can be a big problem at night. Solve the problem by following these three rules of thumb:

- Choose shielded fixtures.
- Place fixtures out of sight lines.
- Lower the overall light levels.

With a shielded fixture, the bulb area is protected by an opaque covering that directs light away from the viewer's eyes. Instead of a hot spot of light, the eye sees the warm glow of the lighted object.

Place shielded fixtures either low (as along a walk) or very high. By doing this properly, you can direct fixtures so that only the light playing in the tree branches is noticed—not a bright glare from the source.

Reduce light levels by using several softer lights, strategically placed around the patio and yard, rather than a single high-wattage bulb.

A little light goes a long way at night. Twenty watts is considered strong, and even 12 watts can be very bright. If a bulb is clearly visible (a porch light in a clear housing, for example), you may find that even a 12-watt refrigerator bulb is adequate for welcoming guests.

Low-voltage or standard current?

Because low-voltage lighting is safer, more energy-efficient, and easier to install than standard 120-volt systems, it is often used outdoors. Low-voltage systems use a transformer to step down household current to 12 volts.

Installing a low-voltage system is relatively simple. Cable can lie on top of the ground, perhaps hidden by mulch or foliage; most fixtures connect easily to cables, and no grounding hookups are required. For more about components, see pages 122–123.

The standard 120-volt system does have some advantages outdoors. The buried cable and metallic fixtures of such an installation give it a look of permanence. Also, light can be projected a great distance, especially useful for increasing security and for lighting trees from ground level. An additional advantage is that power tools and patio heaters can be plugged into 120-volt outdoor outlets.

Setting the stage

Night lighting lets you edit your views; basically, the garden stops where the light stops. Whether your garden is large or small, you should always start by determining how much of it you want to light. It's important to be aware of how your

This garden looks great in daylight (left), but when the sun goes down it really comes alive. Effects include dramatic uplighting below palm and olive trees, downlighting to brighten patio and table, ground-level lighting to highlight planting beds, backlighting behind the potted trees, and wall washing on the end wall and fireplace.

lights might affect the neighbors, too (some communities even have ordinances regulating "light trespass").

If you view your garden as a large outdoor room, you'll see that hedges and fences can act as walls, and trees and arbors as ceilings. The same lighting techniques and tricks that work for a room indoors can help you design the lighting for this outdoor space.

Light can help you create a sense of perspective within your outdoor canvas. Lighting designers do this by dividing a garden into three zones: a foreground, which has relatively mid-level brightness; a middle ground, with low-level light and an interplay of shadows; and a background, often given the brightest light of all in order to draw the eye through the garden.

Lighting for safety and security

Ideally, outdoor lighting should combine safety, security, and style. Safety comes first. With this in mind, examine the driveway, the front walk and steps, the front door, the back door and other house approaches, and the swimming pool or spa, if you have one.

The trick to lighting these areas is to combine efficient light with both adequate shielding and a sense of subtlety. You'll find numerous examples in "Great Lighting Ideas," pages 80–91. For a look at some outdoor fixtures and security lights, see "A Shopper's Guide," pages 120–125.

Photocells, timers, and outdoor motion sensors all save energy by switching security lights on and off automatically. Photocells turn lights on at dusk and back off at dawn; with timers, you set the times. Motion-sensor fixtures stay on for a preset interval after being triggered. For shopping pointers, see pages 124–125.

These decorative garden fixtures not only mark the path; they're stylish, too. Semi-opaque glass shades cut glare to a warm glow.

Decorative techniques

You can use a number of lighting techniques to tie a garden's elements together. The two basic mounting positions are downlighting and uplighting. Of the two, downlighting looks more natural—light comes from above and accents or gently washes areas below—though it can also have a dramatic impact. Uplighting, placing the light source beneath what it's illuminating, is more theatrical. It can be especially useful in new gardens lacking mature trees.

A single, direct source sometimes flattens a lighted object unnaturally, making it look like a billboard. Multiple sources give it dimension. For a dappled, "moonlight" effect, use both uplights and downlights to light a large tree. Decorative rope lights used to outline trees, steps, and railings can lend sparkle to your landscape.

You can create interesting garden effects by placing uplights, downlights, and accent lights on separate switches. Install dimmers (page 118) for even greater flexibility.

What does it take to install new lighting? Replacing an outdated fixture or dimmer with a new one can be a simple half-hour matter of screws, wire nuts, and a screwdriver. When adding a new fixture, though, things get messier: you need to run new electrical cable (shown below) from an existing source to the new location, mount a new fixture box, and then wire in the new fixture and secure it to the box.

■ **Mapping.** Before you add lighting—as opposed to replacing an existing fixture—it's important to know which circuits control which existing fixtures, plug-in outlets, and switches. Some circuits may already be carrying the maximum current allowed by law.

To chart circuits, you'll need a small table lamp or night-light that you can carry around to test plug-in outlets. After turning the first circuit breaker to the OFF position or removing the first fuse, go through the house and check all appliances, switches, and outlets; on a rough map of your house, label those that are now dead with the circuit number.

Repeat the process with each circuit, making sure that you've turned the previous circuit breaker back on or replaced the previous fuse.

Once you've mapped your circuits, you can plan to add fixtures or plug-in outlets to circuits controlled by 15-amp circuit breakers or fuses.

ELECTRICAL CABLE
(TYPE NM)

TECHNICAL TALK

As a rule, a 15-amp circuit can handle a maximum of 1,440 watts. Add up the watts marked on the appliances and bulbs fed by the circuit to which you want to add. Subtract this sum from 1,440 to find out how many watts you can add to the circuit.

If you're confused by load calculations or want to know whether you can tap into a circuit rated at more than 15 amps, call on your local building department's electrical inspector.

■ **Wiring.** Thinking of doing the wiring yourself? The trick is to find a route for new electrical cable. If walls and/or floors and ceilings are exposed, you're in luck. Otherwise, you'll almost certainly need to cut into—then patch and paint—wall and ceiling materials to gain access for cable. For step-by-step planning and wiring details, see the Sunset book *Complete Home Wiring.*

Where cutting into walls, ceilings, and floors to route new wire is too difficult, surface

wiring may be the answer—especially if you're comfortable with the somewhat "industrial" look that results. Surface wiring systems are safe and neat, usually consisting of protective channels and housing boxes (shown at left below) that allow you to mount wiring on practically any wall or ceiling material.

If you do plan to tackle a home wiring project yourself, there's one firm rule: Never work on a "live" circuit. Always remove the fuse or switch the circuit breaker to the OFF position before beginning work.

PENDANT

WIRE NUTS

SURFACE WIRING SYSTEM

ADJUSTABLE FIXTURE BOX

GREAT
LIGHTING
IDEAS

YOU'VE LEARNED THE BASICS— now it's time to get creative. In this chapter we take you on a photo tour of great home lighting ideas, traveling room by room. Along the way you're sure to find styles as well as strategies that will work for you. **WE BEGIN AT THE FRONT DOOR,** wind our way through the living room, kitchen, and dining area, and then move on down the hall to the bedroom, bath, and home office. Finally, it's off to the great outdoors, where we show how good lighting blends sparkle with both safety and security. **BROWSE AT YOUR LEISURE,** perhaps marking your favorite pictures to show to a lighting designer or supplier. If you run across unfamiliar terms, you should be able to find explanations of them in the previous section of this book, "A Planning Primer." See some fixtures or controls you'd like to learn more about? Turn to "A Shopper's Guide," beginning on page 93.

entries

Eᴺᴛʀɪᴇs ᴍᴀᴋᴇ first impressions. Light them warmly and you allow your guests to look their best as you invite them to come on in. Don't overlight: the contrast to the outdoors can be disorienting. Both porch and entry fixtures should be well shielded to minimize glare.

An entry's lighting sets the tone for what lies beyond in your home. The rule for both lighting style and fixtures: *keep it simple*. If you opt for an eye-catching chandelier or pendant, don't add competing focal points. The same goes for accenting display objects and plantings. Add soft fill light, controlled by dimmers, by means of built-in cove lighting, light-diffusing wall sconces, or even an antique table lamp with an opaque shade.

What's the view down the hall? Entry light levels and fixture style should complement the areas that are visible beyond the entry. A focal point or points down a long entryway can lead guests on into the living spaces.

Lighting can make your entry seem bigger or smaller. Stretch an entry's perceived size by uplighting a light-colored ceiling or by spacing fixtures horizontally down a hallway. To make a large space seem more intimate, try spare down-lighting, higher-contrast lighting, pinpoint accenting, or light-diffusing wall sconces positioned low to effectively lower the ceiling line. Mirrors also spread light and create the illusion of more space.

A light for the coat closet and another near a mirror for that last-minute check make entry lighting complete.

A bold entry sports twin cast-metal lamps that flank a stylish mirror and sit atop a demilune table.

There's no glare-producing ceiling fixture here. Instead, the glowing, faux-painted walls are softly lit by indirect ceiling cove lighting, aided by a modern wall sconce. Pinpoint accenting adds punch, courtesy of ceiling-mounted down-lights with aimable eyeball trim.

A streamlined entry previews the ultramodern home design beyond. Lighting is correspondingly clean: hidden downlights accent the framed photos, and a warm glow comes from strip lighting tucked beneath the floating shelf's lip.

Entry mirrors can stretch apparent space and spread available light. This narrow, windowless entry in an urban row house achieves both effects. Wall sconces positioned on the mirror add a warm glow and echo fixtures found throughout the house.

Effective lighting pulls the eye into this entry and down an open hallway that doubles as an art gallery. The zoomy entry sconce sets the tone; paintings are lit by ceiling-mounted downlights with slot apertures. A built-in soffit bounces soft fill light off the ceiling.

living rooms

LIVING SPACES present prime opportunities for flexible, multilayered lighting schemes. You'll want to include well-shielded task lighting for reading or handiwork as well as accent lighting for artwork, collections, or architectural features. Soft, adjustable levels of ambient light set a congenial mood for entertaining or watching television.

Built-in architectural fixtures such as valances, soffits, and coves are effective ambient sources. So are wall sconces, movable torchères, and wall washers. Traditional floor and table lamps are enjoying a renaissance, too, with many new design options on the market and in the works. Remember, though, that these and other decorative fixtures shouldn't carry the lighting load: if turned up high, they're big glare producers. Pharmacy lamps with adjustable necks and built-in dimmers are tops for efficient task lighting.

Discreet downlights can complement both contemporary and traditional styles of decor, but they're best reserved for accenting or for lighting casual tasks. Art and furnishings change over time; choose adjustable downlights that can be adapted for future needs. If you're retrofitting, consider whimsical cable lights or other low-voltage tracks.

Dimmers, panels that control individual lighting scenes, or computer controls let you adjust multiple light sources for varied living-room uses and moods. Floor outlets enable lamp cords to follow furnishings; three- and four-way switches let you access lights as you enter one way and exit another.

Pinpoint downlights handle both ambient and accent lighting needs. These fixtures are meant to be in the background, allowing the decorative neon wall art to take center stage.

Collectibles seem to float within this elegant display cabinet. Recessed downlights shine from the top; backlighting, separately switched, comes from fiber optics behind the translucent back.

Understated colors and accessories are underscored by a matte-black pharmacy lamp—a particularly apt choice for living-room task lighting (especially when supplied with a dimmer).

A beautifully spare living room and the bedroom beyond are highlighted by low-voltage MR-16 downlights with aimable slot apertures. The hallway's smooth, indirect light comes from two dimmable 250-watt quartz wall washers tucked up in the skylight well.

Comfortable and eclectic, this TV room has seemingly casual but highly efficient lighting. The overhead pendant casts diffuse light down and bounce light up, avoiding the glare of a standard ceiling fixture. Discreet downlights with pinhole apertures add "invisible" accents. A paper-shaded corner fixture supplies fun and fill light. Light from an adjacent space is shared through glass blocks.

Lined up along a pedestal shelf surrounding the sunken room, a marching row of tall torchères extends style and ambient light into an otherwise dark area. Torchères are handy, movable alternatives to sconces or other ambient built-ins.

Tall walls—especially those below vaulted ceilings—are made for built-in uplighting. The wall sconces at left, mounted in the high "clerestory" area, shine light up and off the white, angled ceiling, creating lots of soft ambient fill for the living space below.

Soft fill light, harder accenting, and a warm candlelight

glow combine in this inviting living room. The design takes

advantage of open ceiling trusses to hide rows of adjustable

track fixtures. High-mounted wall sconces supply the fill.

Formal but flexible, twin table lamps atop a library desk serve both desk and sofa. Classic candelabra sconces above the fireplace mantel add ambient light as well as decorative sparkle.

Votives in glass holders dance from decorative wrought-iron fixtures, bringing soft light to a garden-room scene.

This retro decor is brought to life by integral banks of
fluorescent fixtures that send ample light both up and down.
Light shines down through mesh-screen covers that serve as
louvers, softening the output and cutting glare. Open above,
these fixtures bounce additional fill light up and off the ceiling.

A curving cable system is an updated alternative to traditional track fixtures. Here, the mini–reflector bulbs handle accenting and wall-washing tasks. Cable systems make easy retrofits for existing ceiling fixtures and can help "liven up" a tall, potentially cold-looking room.

It's not illegal to have fun with light fixtures! This inventive "chandelier," straight from the hardware store, forms the perfect counterpoint to a wall display of junkyard car emblems and a parking-lot mirror. The fixture is fashioned from standard work lights or "clamp lamps" hard-wired into several junction boxes above.

You can accent artwork in many ways. One of the simplest—and least expensive—is with an add-on picture light. The fixture shown here looks traditional and helps artwork appear bolder and shine brighter.

A portable, easy-to-add uplight silhouettes a tall indoor plant and highlights the textures of rough-hewn walls and moldings.

The clean, classic lines of this room shine through, thanks to a sympathetic lighting scheme. Recessed, aimable down-lights handle accent and wall-washing tasks; soffit-mounted display lights shine down through glass-shelved display niches. To counteract all that downlighting, uplights bounce indirect light off the warm wood ceiling.

kitchens

TODAY'S **KITCHEN** is the household hub or "command center." As a gathering place, a kitchen needs flexible lighting for both late-night snacks and full-scale entertaining. And whether there's one cook or a crew of kitchen helpers at work, task lighting for the sink, countertops, and cooktop is essential.

Multiple sources and dimmer controls let you turn light up full-throttle when you're working or down to a warm glow after hours.

You'll want strong, shadowless light right over each kitchen work area. In most cases, shielded strip lights under the cabinets—hidden behind a trim strip or valance—are the best way to light counter areas. Downlights effectively illuminate the sink and work islands.

Surface-mounted fixtures, once a kitchen mainstay, are now used specifically to draw attention to themselves. Hanging pendants are especially popular; place them over a breakfast nook or an island—or anywhere they won't present a traffic hazard.

Fluorescent tubes are unrivaled for energy efficiency; they also last far longer than incandescent bulbs. In some energy-conscious areas, general lighting for new kitchens *must* be fluorescent. Though fixture options for fluorescent bulbs and tubes are limited, indirect treatments using them are popular: the tubes are placed in soffits atop cabinets or in overhead coves.

Kitchen task lighting is often delivered by means of under-cabinet strip lights. Here they're sealed and softened within frosted acrylic panels on cabinet bottoms.

The owner of this kitchen, part of a remodeled winery, wanted lots of light, but the raised ceiling made it a tough task. Stylish red Italian pendants housing tiny but efficient quartz bulbs solved the problem and defined the space. Electrical conduit, painted white, leads from the roofline down to the fixtures, which were designed to be ceiling-mounted.

An eclectic, casual kitchen
sports casual, "unfitted" lighting
to match, including two chain-
hung glass pendants, table
lamps, and even a jaunty string
of Christmas lights. Sure, it's less
efficient than some schemes,
but it's more fun.

Three glass-and-chrome
pendants follow the line of the
butcher-block prep island.
Downlights mark the rear
countertop; decorative uplights
in high cabinet soffits add
background fill.

While many designers chafe against energy requirements that demand fluorescents in kitchens, the architect of this space reveled in the look—finding them the perfect touch for a retro 50s design. Overhead lighting is flaunted, courtesy of a 36-inch, soffit-mounted ceiling globe. Tubes behind wall cabinets graze the concrete-block wall, and more tubes bounce light off the painted wood ceiling. The lighting is classic "cool" fluorescent throughout.

Need to add light where there's limited overhead access? These surface-mounted, low-voltage track fixtures include integral transformers and add a gleaming look to a high-tech kitchen. Just be sure your cabinet doors will clear the tracks you choose!

No, it's not the War of the Worlds, just fluorescents meeting the future. Except for the trio of tiny pendants hovering near the eating counter, all ceiling fixtures here house space-saving PL-fluorescent tubes.

A hollow central "beam" houses recessed downlights and follows the work surfaces of a hard-working island, shining strong quartz lighting where it's most needed. Track fixtures supply the general lighting; tucked along open ceiling beams, they were custom-colored to blend with the surroundings.

Kitchen schemes rarely feature purely decorative effects, but this one fills the bill. Incandescent mini-tracks run through the soffit area above the wall cabinets, back-lighting bundled dried twigs. This provides enough ambient light to negotiate the kitchen at night when other sources are switched off.

Undercabinet task lighting doubles here as accent light, show-casing a bold glass-mosaic backsplash.

dining areas

T HE FOCUS HERE is the dining table, which can be lit by a traditional chandelier, modern pendants, recessed down-lights—or, even better, some combination of these.

The proportions of a dining-table light fixture in relation to its surroundings are critical. To keep diners or passersby from bumping into it, a hanging fixture should be at least 12 inches narrower than the table. Hanging it about 30 inches above the table surface will help cut down on reflected glare from the tabletop.

Good things can come in threes—like these blown-glass pendants, a decorative departure from the traditional chandelier.

A decorative fixture like a chandelier should *not* be the only light source—it's sure to cause discomfort from glare when turned up. Instead, augment a decorative fixture with one or more adjustable downlights that really do the work. Dimmers can be a real plus—turned up high, the light aids in the task of setting the table or directing guests; turned low, the gentle beam creates a festive atmosphere and minimizes glare. In order to dispel harsh glare and shadows, augment your table lighting with softer fill light on the walls or ceiling. Ambient options include built-in cove lighting, wall sconces, and movable torchères. Accent light on paintings or inside display niches can double as ambient fill, too.

A separate set of fixtures over a buffet will supply light for serving as well as providing background light at mealtimes. Traditional candelabra-style fixtures and modern wall sconces are both popular choices, depending on the room's decor.

Dimmable eyeball MR-16s are the workhorses here, recessed in hollow box beams above the large dining table. Wall sconces flank a built-in buffet, supplying glare-free ambient wash. Candles add decorative glow for formal occasions.

A three-tiered paper shade makes a handsome dining-room accent, doubling as a centerpiece while cutting a hanging pendant's glare-prone output. Staggered wall sconces add fill light while echoing the angle formed by the nearby staircase.

A classic chandelier provides sparkle, not glare; most light comes from the hard-working cove overhead. Four eyeball-trimmed downlights add even accent across the wall screen.

Three beaded pendants hang from low-voltage cables, marking the line of a sturdy waxed-pine dining table. Fixed table lamps are mounted in window alcoves flanking the far fireplace; MR-16 monospots wash fir-paneled walls, lending ambient fill to middle zones. Display cabinets are backlit with strip lights tucked behind rear valances.

A row of modern glass pendants follows the dining-room table; each halogen fixture includes a frosted diffusing ring to minimize glare. The sculptural room divider beyond houses sparkling, end-lit fiber optics inside each niche.

Candles form the focal point (above), while more modern sources— tucked away—contribute accent lighting. Beam-housed fixtures (right) bounce warm light down off the wood ceiling.

hallways and stairs

Hallways may be slim passageways, art galleries, or even glassed-in open areas. But as routes for human traffic, they should be neither much dimmer nor much brighter than adjoining rooms so that your eyes don't have to make big adjustments as you move from room to room.

When planning hall lighting, keep it simple. Downlights are popular here, as are tracks and opaque pendants. If the hall is wide enough, consider spaced wall sconces. A hallway can make an exciting gallery for art, but be sure the light is dimmable—or consider a second set of fixtures for soft illumination, or night-lights for late-night path lighting.

If you have a full staircase—or even just two steps to another level—it's important to provide adequate light for safety. The edge of each tread and the depth of each step should be clearly defined. One way to achieve this is to combine a downlight over the stairs (to light edges) with a softer light pro-jected from the landing below (to define the depth). Another option is to build low-voltage fixtures into the wall just above every third or fourth step. Lights hidden in a handrail can also illuminate treads. For a main landing or entry stairs, consider decora-tive and accent options as well.

For either halls or stairs, plan to install three- or four-way switches at each end or hallway opening; a dimmer can replace one switch for decora-tive lighting control.

Part warehouse, part nautical in mood, these recessed wall lights help mark the way down concrete stair risers. Downlights fill in from overhead.

Lighting a nonlinear central hallway required something new in tracks: a curved, custom statement. The elegant pewter track blends well with the softly faux-painted walls, while the "lily" shades, each with its own MR-16 spot, accent ranks of framed prints.

Glowing mini-lights on a remote transformer light the display niche in the foreground, while an MR-16 monospot illuminates the stair-side niche. Adjustable downlights wash the walls with light.

A curving, low-voltage cable system follows the ins and outs of an upstairs art collection. All that accent light adds ambient hallway light, too, as it bounces off the art and the white walls. A track-mounted globe pendant dives down the stair-well, brightening the space below.

Translucent glass stair treads, shown here from below, seem to glow. The light really comes from MR-16 bulbs tucked inside the built-in, recessed wall rectangles.

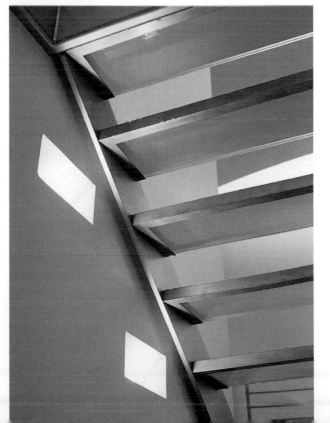

bedrooms

ONCE THE REALM of a glare-producing ceiling globe and clunky plug-in table lamps, the bedroom is now the setting for major news in lighting design. Multiple, dimmable light sources can add welcome flexibility—especially useful for today's open master-suite schemes.

On the subtle end of the bedroom lighting scale, soft ambient levels create a quiet aura. Decorative sconces, torchères, or built-in cove lighting can provide soft, glare-free fill light. If you're replacing an existing ceiling globe, consider an opaque pendant that directs light up and off the ceiling. Check to ensure that glare won't be a problem for someone reclining in bed: overhead fixtures should be carefully aimed and fitted, as needed, with tight trim covers and baffles or louvers. And be sure the bedroom fixtures and bulbs you choose produce minimal noise or "hum."

Bright, directional reading lights on either side of a bed allow one person to sleep while the other reads into the wee hours. Such fixtures should be adjustable and well shielded. Or use a pair of dimmable low-voltage downlights, cross-aimed like overhead airline lights to prevent shadows.

A bedside switch to turn off main room lights is handy. A second switch can control night-lights. A recent innovation is a bedside master switch to control computerized security lights both indoors and out.

The pewter bedside light in this guest room has been custom-fitted to a mounting block; it rides up and down the post of a steel canopy bed, tightening with the turn of a brass knob.

There's a soft look overall here— appropriate for a master bedroom—but it's built up from several flexible sources. Recessed downlights with aimable slot apertures direct ambient wall-wash to the headboard area. Monospots with honey-combed louvers create tight, low-glare accents on paintings. A pair of bedside task lamps provides adjustable light for reading.

A multilayered lighting scheme, usually reserved
for formal living rooms, comes to this master-suite
conversation space. Punchy PAR downlights wash the
fireplace; low-voltage downlights pinpoint mirror and
mantel. Strip lights tucked behind a ceiling cove furnish
ambient fill. There's more accent lighting inside the
display cases. A table lamp lends a cozy, traditional
feel and ample reading light.

"Classic but clean" was the plan, and recessed
downlights helped carry it out. General lighting is via
dimmable PAR lights with polished reflectors; smaller
MR-16s with louvers spotlight planters. When it's time
for relaxing, the downlights are turned off, leaving the
soft indirect glow from strip lights in the coved ceiling
(they're hidden behind classic crown moldings).

great lighting ideas

It doesn't need to be complicated! The spare design at right keeps the light—and the overall bedroom look—simple, shapely, and colorful. Matching reading lamps offer bedside task light; a pair of wall sconces adds style and fill light. Fixture shapes and colors are echoed in the wall art.

This minimalist bedroom scheme includes no night table, so it features an articulating reading lamp (with its own switch) housed inside the recessed headboard. Low, wall-recessed lights mark the path from bed to bath; they can be turned on separately for soft fill or to guide a late-night bed-to-bath stroll.

The closets in this basement bedroom are faced with translucent, sliding shoji panels that match an overall Oriental theme—and add soft ambient light. The glowing panels are lit from behind and are washed from the front by downlights fitted with slot apertures.

bathrooms

THE NUMBER ONE TRICK to lighting bathrooms effectively is to provide task light that's gently flattering yet strong enough for grooming. Lights around a mirror used for shaving or applying makeup should spread light over a person's face rather than onto the mirror surface. To avoid heavy shadows, place lights at the sides rather than only at the top of the bathroom mirror.

Popular solutions include theater makeup bars, wall sconces, and tubes mounted vertically. Some mirror units have integral tubes, inset light diffusers, or swing-out makeup mirrors with their own light source. Choose warm-toned tubes or bulbs for accurate makeup light and good skin tones.

Because they are the most energy-efficient choice, fluorescent lights are required for general bathroom lighting in some locales. Indirect sources work well here: consider cove and soffit lighting, translucent diffusers, and other "bounce" lighting to spread a soft, even level of illumination.

Tub, shower, and toilet compartments may need their own light fixtures. Bath and shower lights must be sealed and approved for wet locations. Any light fixture within reach of water should be protected by a GFCI (ground fault circuit interrupter) to prevent electrical shock.

Multiple light sources and multiple controls allow you to alternate between morning efficiency and nighttime serenity. Consider dimmers here. Also plan to provide low-energy night lighting for safety and convenience.

A fluorescent ring surrounds the mirror above a stylish pedestal sink. The fixture supplies even grooming light from all directions.

During daylight hours, decorative glass is a source of discreet ambient light; at night, one wall is washed by a bank of angled downlights with slot apertures. At the mirror, a glareproof frosted wall sconce provides efficient side light for grooming; a downlight fills in from above. The undercounter glow is just for fun.

This master bath features a long vanity with hand-tooled
marble top and a matching mirror cabinet broken by
flush-mounted, vertical incandescent tubes for even makeup lighting. The backsplash and counter are washed by
additional light from the cabinet's bottom edge.

While lighting was kept intentionally spare in the modern bath shown below, it maximizes both task and decorative opportunities. At the mirror, a diffused inset fixture gives just the right amount of makeup light. The lighted niche at right glows with warm fluorescent light that passes through the diffusing panel between open and closed storage areas. Through another opening, the niche glows as a decorative "night-light" for the hallway beyond.

Twin wall sconces flank the chestlike wood mirror frame, providing warm, welcoming grooming light in a small powder room. The glass-block wall passes available light around the windowless space, adding decoration and a mottled, shimmering light.

Workaday, sinkside porcelain wall sockets retain some of their down-home feel but are dressed up and shielded by "lodge-style" twigs supporting translucent diffusers.

A powder room showcases a handpainted pedestal sink, brash black-and-white marble, and—embedded in diamond-shaped floor accents—a decorative flourish of fiber-optic lighting. A garage below yielded a home for the lighting tubes, which shine up through glass inserts in the subfloor.

work spaces

THE FIRST DESIGN RULE for today's home office is this: *don't* make it look like an office. In other words, choose both your interior decor and your light fixtures to complement the surrounding living spaces within your home.

When arranging light fixtures and choosing bulbs, make sure that your work surface will be free of heavy shadows, which can cause eyestrain. By combining diffuse ambient lighting and adjustable task lighting, you can avoid overly strong contrasts between a work area and the rest of a room.

Fluorescent built-ins, wall washers, and wall sconces are effective for fill lighting. A PL-fluorescent or halogen task lamp—or a fixture that combines the two—is effective for close work.

Glare is a potential problem, especially around a computer screen. A screen shade or glare guard can help shield your monitor. Adjust screen illumination to match the room lighting level, and turn up the contrast. It's best if lighting—including natural light—comes from the side; light behind the monitor can cause eyestrain, while light in front can bounce glare off the screen.

Light-colored blotters on dark-finished desks and light-hued walls and ceiling will reflect light back onto your work. But a wall or ceiling that's too bright may throw glare onto your computer screen. One solution: place ambient lights on dimmers, then dial them up or down as needed, depending on the task at hand.

A rustic home office sports two pharmacy lamps mounted on bookcase walls; recessed downlights with slot apertures; and larger, open-trim downlights and uplights in bookcase soffits.

Unlike standard track fixtures, some cable lights can follow curves—in this case, the line of a custom-built desk. A wall sconce creates ambient fill and reinforces the idea that this is a home, not just an office. The little halogen fixture on the desk is primarily decorative.

A dark attic office has a pair of traditional, movable desk lamps to match its impeccable Craftsman detailing. When you need close, shadow-free task light, two sources are better than one.

The lighting here was designed to look "soft," in contrast to the hard, industrial concrete and stone. A low-voltage cable system follows the curve of the desk alcove above floating maple shelves; aluminum louvers control light spill and add style. For ambient fill, the stone wall is grazed by light from a string of reflector lamps hidden inside a light well.

Subtle, multilayered lighting comes to the home office. It begins here with a traditional ceiling fixture, but this one diffuses light for more ambient ceiling bounce and less glare. Strip lights above and below the bookcase illuminate the counter and add a decorative glow on top; downlights over the window shine onto the counter there and wash window coverings. Primary task lighting comes from a tabletop lamp.

When was the last time you saw a laundry room with good lighting?
This one has plenty of general light for moving around and seeing
inside cabinets, thanks to recessed downlights with diffusing lenses.
They're coupled with efficient fluorescent undercabinet task lighting.

You wouldn't call this just a home office. For starters,
there's the eye-popping ceiling pendant—and then
there's accent light from inside the glass-fronted cabinets
and from tracks partly hidden by a ceiling valance.
A compact lamp takes over for desktop tasks.

*How do you light a tall, open studio space? One way is to
effectively lower the ceiling by lowering the fixtures—in this
case, sturdy traditional tracks suspended from vertical
feeds off overhead ceiling boxes.*

outdoor ideas

Garden path lights can be garden decor, too—day or night. This fixture has a handblown glass shade "flower" and a patinaed copper "stem."

SAFETY AND SECURITY are the starting points for outdoor lighting schemes, but new designs fold these into subtle, decorative landscaping plans. Glare and harsh point sources are outdoor bugaboos. Be sure that light sources are shielded; it's best if they're not seen at all. Multiple light sources are much better than a single glaring flood or clear-glass point source. Basic techniques for successful outdoor lighting are outlined on pages 22–25.

Driveways—especially if they're long and wooded—should have some kind of low, soft lights to define their boundaries. The garage area needs security lighting, preferably controlled by switches both inside and out. Motion-sensitive fixtures mounted on a garage are also useful; for details, see page 124.

Front walks and steps are easiest to light if their surfaces are a light, reflective color. Low fixtures that spread soft pools of light can guide guests and at the same time highlight your garden's virtues along the walkway. If your house has deep eaves or an overhang that extends the length of your walk, consider installing weatherproof downlights. Even single steps should be illuminated if they're any distance from the door.

At the front door, you'll want light to serve several purposes. Besides illuminating your house number and welcoming guests, it should provide sufficient brightness for you to see a caller's face. If you choose decorative fixtures of clear glass at the front door, keep low-wattage bulbs in them to avoid uncomfortable brightness.

(Continued on page 82)

Viewed through the open gate, this inviting entry corridor has equally inviting lighting. Shielded eye-level lights shine both up and down off arbor and stone columns, while arbor eaves house uplighting and some well-placed downlights. At the far end, the interior entry light glows warmly through decorative glass doors.

On decks and patios, a low level of light is often enough for quiet conversation or alfresco dining. By lighting steps, railings, or benches from underneath—or directly, with strip lights—you can outline the edges of your structure for safety. Don't forget to add stronger light wherever you do your serving or barbecuing. Downlights are a popular choice for this, but indirect lighting—diffused through plastic or another translucent material—is also useful.

Light swimming pools and spas for safety and also to make them attractive from inside the house. To avoid glare off the water, consider putting pool lights on a dimmer. For relaxing and entertaining, all the light that's needed is a soft glow to outline the water's edges, but the light should be at full brightness when children are swimming. A spa or garden pool can be illuminated with low-voltage strip lights that will subtly outline its perimeter or steps. Water and electricity don't mix—when planning these systems, it's best to get professional help.

Uplighting, downlighting, and backlighting (see pages 12–13) are all effective ways to light foliage. Decorative mini-lights lend sparkle to trees, shrubs, and outdoor structures. Be aware that plant species and type (deciduous or evergreen) will affect the spread of light. Translucent foliage transmits light; dense leaves drink it up. And keep in mind that unless you prune regularly, your lighting effects will change significantly as plantings mature. Conversely, fixture and bulb spread can dramatically alter landscaping effects; so can the use of colored filters.

Here's an easy and subtle way to add night light to a patio fence: a hollow wood sleeve with a low-voltage light built into the top. The unit slips over any tall 4-by-4 post, leaving enough room for the power cord.

A long, shielded fluorescent fixture safely lights the entry walkway while highlighting a garden bench and the rough concrete wall behind. Large windows and skylights add light from inside the house.

The house itself can be a glowing light source, both decorative and welcoming. This translucent overhead marks the front entry; it's lit by wall-mounted downlights from above, casting a warm glow across the entry deck below.

A wide-open house plan that intentionally
bridges inside and outside living areas calls for
good outdoor lighting, too. Living-space lighting
here features efficient monospots and floor lamps.
Outside the telescoping French doors, a sitting area
is highlighted by crisp halogen downlighting and
accented, for fun, with low-voltage rope lights
tied to the copper-clad arbor.

Outdoor grazing highlights stone and wood textures here, adding ambient light and minimizing
glare. Post-mounted arbor lights shine both up and
down but are shielded at eye level.

*In a whimsically splayed line-
up, classic candle lanterns tilt
to and fro along winding garden steps; they're both
functional and festive.*

*Special occasions such as holidays or outdoor
parties may call for temporary lighting.
Classic Mexican luminarias—open paper bags
that contain votive candles set in sand—have now
been electrified. A broad range of lanterns is also
available, from hurricane lamps that burn oil to
glass-sided lanterns that house candles.*

*Path lights to mark direction and distance at night can
look great, too—witness the unusual fixtures above. Choose
between bold, bright standard-voltage fixtures and smaller,
low-voltage options; the latter can be repositioned until you
get things just right.*

This octagonal umbrella casts cooling shade by day and warm, reflected light by night. Four bulbs nestle at the top of the center pole, bouncing a soft glow off the umbrella and back down below.

At night, the view ends where the light ends, but this forest of
oaks and madrones presents a multilayered drama, thanks to
careful fixture placement. The 150-watt, standard-voltage uplights
are mounted to deck fascias; softer downlights for foot traffic are
attached to house siding and fitted with glare-reducing louvers.
The strong light penetrates tinted windows, allowing the owners
to view the trees from inside the house.

*Recessed, sealed well lights graze colorful concrete walls, forming a soft, textured backdrop
for alfresco dining. Candles add their warm, decorative glow atop the table.*

*The homeowners stretched their
indoor space by fashioning this outdoor "living room," complete with
a lighting scheme that echoes indoor
lighting. Fluorescent wall sconces
provide ambient light; plantings
are accented with buried halogen
uplights. Each colorful tile cube is
backlit by its own step light; safety
lights mark stair risers. Pool and
waterfall are highlighted by two
submersible pool lights.*

This naturalistic garden pond features a combination of subtle light sources. Uplights tucked into rocks accent water plants, while submerged pool lights create the water's glow and show off the waterfall shelf.

Punchy uplights accent massive oaks, reflected in a quiet, shimmering swimming pool; other discreet fixtures paint surrounding plantings. The pool should have its own lights, separately controlled, for safe swimming.

A classical poolside loggia is ready for a quiet summer evening's repose. Above the dining table, a hanging candelabra with votive candles produces a soft glow; it's augmented with a central downlight above. Accent light comes from 75-watt reflector bulbs housed in arbor-mounted downlights; two flank the back of each column, backlighting them dramatically. The water's glow is the result of two wall-mounted pool fixtures.

A SHOPPER'S GUIDE

YOU'VE SEEN what great lighting can do. Now it's time to take a closer look at the hardware that makes it happen. Some devices stay quietly in the background, while some just beg to be noticed. Bulbs come first, then the fixtures that house them and shape the light. Controls—a catchall phrase for a slew of switches, dimmers, and timers—are also a big part of today's flexible schemes. **AND LIGHTING TECHNOLOGY** doesn't stop indoors. For gardens, patios, and pools, choose from punchy 120-volt or sparkling low-voltage effects. Outdoor controls like photocells, timers, and motion sensors add both convenience and security. **WHERE DO YOU GET** all these products? Increasingly, you'll find a sizable selection at home improvement centers; for outdoor products, check garden centers and landscape suppliers. Lighting showrooms and "light labs" handle the zoomier styles and let you see your options in action. Lighting professionals and electricians can help with the fine points, such as low-voltage logistics, wiring practicalities, high-end controls, and "smart-house" strategies.

Incandescent Bulbs

THE OLD STANDBYS

Incandescent light, the kind we're most familiar with, is produced by a tungsten filament that burns slowly inside a glass bulb (shown on page 18). Incandescent light has a warm, comfortable glow that gets even warmer when it's dimmed.

Incandescent bulbs are inexpensive and easy to find; they fit a wide variety of fixture types and styles. They're also easy to dim using standard dimmers (see page 118).

On the minus side, incandescent is the least energy-efficient light source now available, and it tends not to last as long as other sources. For a closer look at how various light types stack up, see "Bulb Comparisons at a Glance" on pages 102–103.

A-BULBS are the old incandescent standbys; they actually date back to the 1800s. As shown below, A-bulbs come in clear, frosted, and colored versions (including skin-flattering pink and a new blue-coated "daylight" bulb). The light emitted from an A-bulb spreads in all directions—it's the fixture or shade that shapes the light.

A-bulb sizes include A15, A17, A19, A21, and A23. (For a translation, see "Speaking in Code" on the facing page.) Common wattages range from 15 to 250 watts.

R-BULB

Three-way bulbs, which fit special floor and table lamps, have twin filaments that combine to produce switchable spreads from 30/70/100 to 100/200/300 watts.

R (REFLECTOR) BULBS brought directional accent lighting to the residential scene when they were first introduced in the 1950s. Internal aluminized reflectors allowed them to project light forward, paving the way for two now-classic fixtures: tracks and recessed downlights. By today's standards, though, R-bulbs are big and bulky; more important, they're now considered energy hogs—so much so that they're being phased out. The similarly shaped PAR bulb is generally much more efficient, and while there are incandescent PAR bulbs out there, most are now halogen (for details, see page 99).

A-BULBS

GLOBE-SHAPED BULB

FLAME-SHAPED BULBS

TWIN-PIN BASE BULB

The ER (ellipsoidal reflector) bulb actually focuses light a few inches in front of the bulb, so it "bites" better than the regular R-bulb, allowing equal impact for fewer watts.

SB (SILVERED-BOWL) BULBS are shaped like A-bulbs, but their silvered caps cut glare and provide some indirect light when used in pendants, track fixtures, and downlights.

T (TUBULAR) BULBS are, yes, tube-shaped. Available in clear and frosted versions, they're used in pharmacy lamps, task lamps, under-cabinet strips, and picture lights.

DECORATIVE BULBS—those meant to be seen—are still incandescent's strong suit. Traditional chandeliers and sconces usually sport clear or frosted flame-shaped bulbs; some pendants call for globe-shaped bulbs. Most larger decorative types of bulbs have the standard "medium screw base"; others have smaller screw bases, and some have twin-pin bases (shown above right).

INCANDESCENT TUBES, producing a warm, even glow that flatters skin tones, look like fluorescents (see page 97). Unlike fluorescents, though, these tubes are expensive—and they won't last nearly as long.

SB-BULB

T-BULBS

SPEAKING IN CODE

Light bulbs are sometimes identified with a terse numbering system that seems obscure, but it's actually simple to crack. Here's an example:

50WR30

The code works like this: wattage + bulb shape abbreviation + diameter. In this case, it's a 50-watt R-bulb that's $30/8$ inches in diameter.

It's $30/8$ inches in diameter? Yes, the numbers given for size are in $1/8$-inch increments, so a size 30 is about $3\frac{3}{4}$ inches across. An A19 A-bulb measures about $2\frac{3}{8}$ inches across.

Sometimes a code for beam spread or pattern is tagged onto the end. If the listing says "50WR30FL," the FL stands for "flood." VNSP means "very narrow spot."

Fluorescent Tubes and Bulbs

GREAT NEW SHAPES AND COLORS

Though renowned for both energy efficiency and long life, fluorescent light still got no respect—until recently.

Early fluorescents were notorious for hum, flicker, and unpleasant color rendering. Better fixtures and fixture ballasts (integral voltage regulators) have largely remedied the first two problems; new tube technology has vastly expanded color options. And while fixture designs for traditional tubes are still limited, new compact fluorescent bulbs are impacting fixture styling.

Fluorescents diffuse light evenly in all directions, so they're great for broad, ambient light or for close-at-hand tasks. Cool operating temperatures and long life make them excellent for hard-to-vent, hard-to-reach soffits, coves, and other architectural built-ins. Fluorescents

COMPACT FLUORESCENTS

COMPARING ENERGY REQUIREMENTS	
Incandescent Bulbs (watts)	Compact Fluorescents (watts)
40	10
60	15
75	20
100	25

won't, however, provide much accent punch. And they're trickier to dim than both halogen (see pages 98–99) and incandescent, requiring a dimmable fixture ballast and a matching fluorescent dimmer.

FLUORESCENT TUBES (pictured on facing page) come in four basic diameters: T-2, T-5, T-8, and T-12. Remember that bulb/tube diameters are usually specified in $\frac{1}{8}$-inch increments; thus the popular T-12 size is about $1\frac{1}{2}$ inches across. Tubes commonly come in lengths from about 12 inches to 6 feet. You'll need to buy the right pin configuration for your fixture: for example, single-pin, recessed pin, or twin-pin, as shown on the facing page. You'll also need to match the tube to your fixture's ballast—either preheat or rapid-start.

Besides energy-conscious improvements to fluorescent tubes (especially in the T-8 size), the big news is color temperature. Once limited basically to cool white or warm white, fluorescents now come in a dizzying spectrum of colors from very warm (2,700°K) to distinctly cool (6,300°K)—allowing you to match other lights and to choose the effect that suits your taste

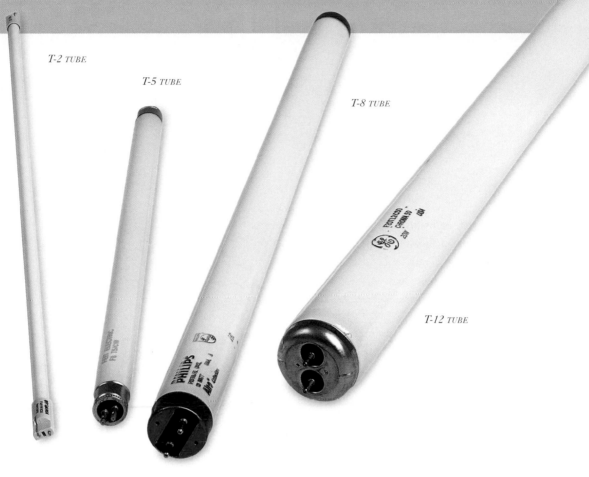

T-2 TUBE

T-5 TUBE

T-8 TUBE

T-12 TUBE

and your decor. For a closer look at the color spectrum, see pages 14–15.

PL-FLUORESCENTS look like small traditional tubes that have been bent back

PL-FLUORESCENTS

on themselves, allowing fluorescent light to be used in smaller, trimmer fixtures—recessed down-lights, for instance. PL-fluorescents come in both twin-tube and quad-tube versions, in a variety of wattages and color temperatures.

CIRCLINE TUBE

CIRCLINE TUBES fit rounded ceiling fixtures and pendants, providing an energy-efficient, ambient alternative to incandescent A-bulbs. Older circline tubes had pin connections, but newer versions screw right into standard light sockets. The circline tube shown above is suitable for any fixture big enough to accept it.

COMPACT FLUORESCENTS (CFLs) directly replace incandescent A-bulbs: they have built-in ballasts and screw bases, so you simply screw a CFL's medium-size base into a standard fixture socket. Some CFLs resemble ordinary A-bulbs or globes; others have exposed tubes bent into a U shape or a coil. CFLs may be too big for some ceiling fixtures. For these, you can use the flatter circline tube.

The table on the facing page shows the energy requirements (watts) of incandescent bulbs and CFLs that produce comparable brightness (usually expressed in lumens). CFLs produce 40 to 60 lumens per watt compared with 8 to 18 lumens for incandescent bulbs.

Halogen Bulbs

BRIGHT WHITE LIGHT

Quartz halogen bulbs, also called tungsten, contain a halogen gas that produces a brighter, whiter beam than other light sources. This recipe also enables halogen bulbs to dramatically outlast their incandescent cousins. Though they don't rival fluorescents for longevity, halogens are unmatched for intensive task lighting, pinpoint accenting, and other dramatic effects. Often they are low voltage, but some halogens use standard line current.

Is there a down side? A halogen bulb gets very hot, and it must be used in fixtures specifically designed and approved for it. The bulbs can be pricey and awkward to handle (see sidebar, facing page), and specialized bulbs used in some fixtures can be hard to find. And even though halogen bulbs burn "white" at full throttle, they still turn a warmish yellow, like incandescents, when dimmed.

MR-11 BULB

MR-16 BULB

PAR BULBS

MR-16 AND MR-11 (MULTI-REFLECTOR) BULBS create the tightest beams. Originally made for movie projectors, these tiny bulbs journeyed to residential use via museum and display lighting, allowing fixture sizes to shrink dramatically. These halogens are used extensively in today's discreet low-voltage downlights, low-voltage tracks, modern pendants, and whimsical cable lights.

MR-16 and MR-11 bulbs come in a wattage range from 20 to 75 and also in a broad spread of beam patterns, including very narrow spot, narrow spot, narrow flood, flood, and wide flood.

Perhaps in a nod to their original use, these bulbs tend to be given their own three-letter abbreviation system instead of the standard wattage/shape/size/spread code of other bulbs. For example, an EZX bulb is a 20-watt MR-16 with a 7-degree spot pattern. The same bulb with a 40-degree flood pattern is called a BAB!

HALOGEN SPECIALTY BULBS

HANDLING HALOGENS

The oils on our hands don't agree with the coatings on halogen bulbs, so it's important to not touch these bulbs directly. Dirty bulbs can crack—or even explode!

Instead, grip new halogen bulbs gently with gloves or a clean rag while installing them. If you do come in contact with the glass, try cleaning the spot with alcohol. Remember that halogen burns very hot, so use care when replacing a newly blown bulb.

PAR (PARABOLIC ALUMINIZED REFLECTOR) BULBS are bigger and punchier than MR-16s; choose them when you need a longer reach and wider coverage. Sizes range from PAR-20 to PAR-38 and wattages from 35 to 250. The large sweep in available wattage reflects the fact that some PAR bulbs are low voltage, while other, larger ones are standard line voltage. The popular PAR-36 bulbs are low voltage only, while PAR-38s are standard voltage.

Like MR-11s and MR-16s, PAR bulbs come in a variety of beam patterns, from very narrow spot through very wide flood. Oblong- or ovoid-shaped patterns are also available.

Some PAR bulbs, particularly low-voltage PAR-36 bulbs, can produce a hum—especially when dimmed. One solution is to install low-voltage fixtures with remote external rather

than integral transformers (see page 115) and place the transformers outside the actual living space.

HALOGEN SPECIALTY BULBS, from tube shapes to tiny Christmas lights, complete a host of halogen fixtures from torchères and pendants to high-intensity task lamps and under-cabinet strips. Heat buildup can be a problem here, so be sure to use the exact bulb specified for the fixture.

XENON BULBS are new, cooler-burning spin-offs of halogen. Their tiny size and extra-long life span make them naturals for strip-light applications (see pages 110-111). They're great for small, recessed display lights and under-cabinet task fixtures. Also look for xenon in hard-to-reach built-ins such as coves and soffits.

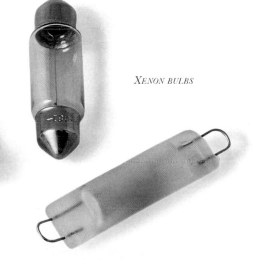

XENON BULBS

Specialty Sources

PART ART, PART INDUSTRY

Though incandescents, fluorescents, and halogen bulbs are the workhorses of home lighting, several other light sources are gaining a foothold, too. Some, like neon and HID, have been around for a while; others, notably fiber optics, are up-and-coming stars. Look for improved, updated versions of all these sources in the coming years.

Neon

This zoomy light source, bringing to mind 1950s casino and bar signs, is generated when electricity passes through a gas. Neon gas, to be specific, glows orange-red (other gases give off a variety of colors). Neon's low light output makes it undesirable as a functional light source, but it can be bent into all sorts of decorative, sculptural shapes.

Requiring a 24-volt transformer, neon fixtures can be expensive to buy, though they don't use much energy and may last for years. Newer transformers have reduced the sometimes objectionable buzz emitted from older neon sources.

Neon for home lighting is sold primarily as freestanding pieces through individual artisans or lighting showrooms.

Cold cathode

Long-lasting cold cathode shines in contoured, confined quarters where other sources fear to tread. Its typical white light is brighter than neon, making it more useful for ambient lighting, and its custom-shaping capability offers decorative flourish.

Cold cathode is often the high-end light of choice for indirect, architectural use and for inaccessible coves and valances where changing shorter-lived bulbs or tubes presents a major challenge. Think of it as fluorescent that can follow a curve.

NEON

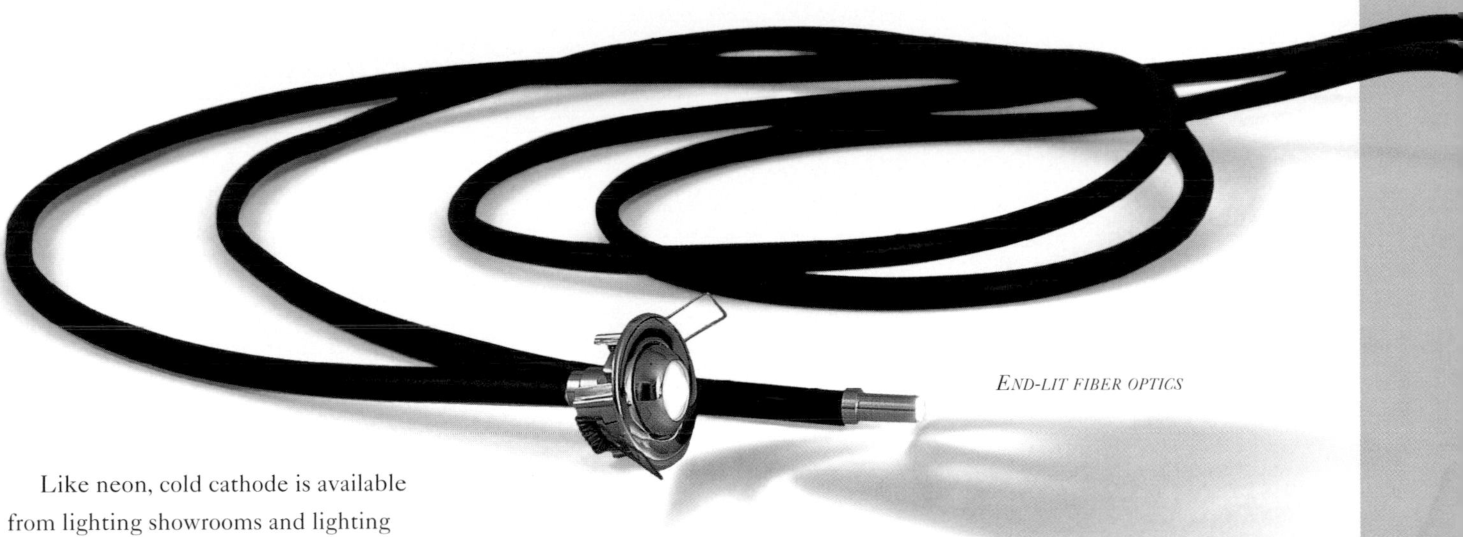

END-LIT FIBER OPTICS

Like neon, cold cathode is available from lighting showrooms and lighting designers.

Fiber optics

Really a vehicle rather than a light source, fiber optics carry light or other media (such as data signals) as if through a tunnel. Put a light source such as halogen or metal halide at one end, and the glass or plastic fiber tubing will beam it efficiently toward the other. End-lit fiber optics shine bright light out the end of opaque fiber cable; edge-lit versions shine all the way along transparent tubing. On one hand, fiber optics function as a decorative alternative to neon or cold cathode, following contoured shapes at will. Unlike neon or cold cathode, however, fiber optics will transmit any color, by shining the light through colored filters. Fiber optics excel in several other ways, too: the end-lit fiber cable can go places ordinary electrical cable can't, and it can be covered over; and because there's no electrical current passing through the cable itself, it's a natural to use around water, indoors and out.

On the down side, fiber optics are still quite expensive, and they can be tricky to connect.

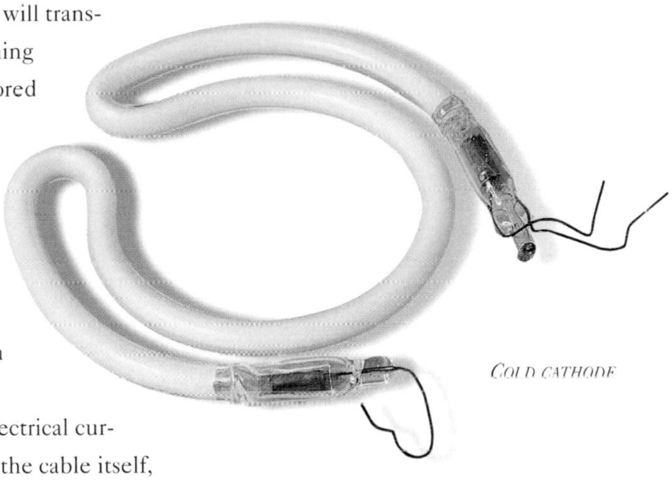

COLD CATHODE

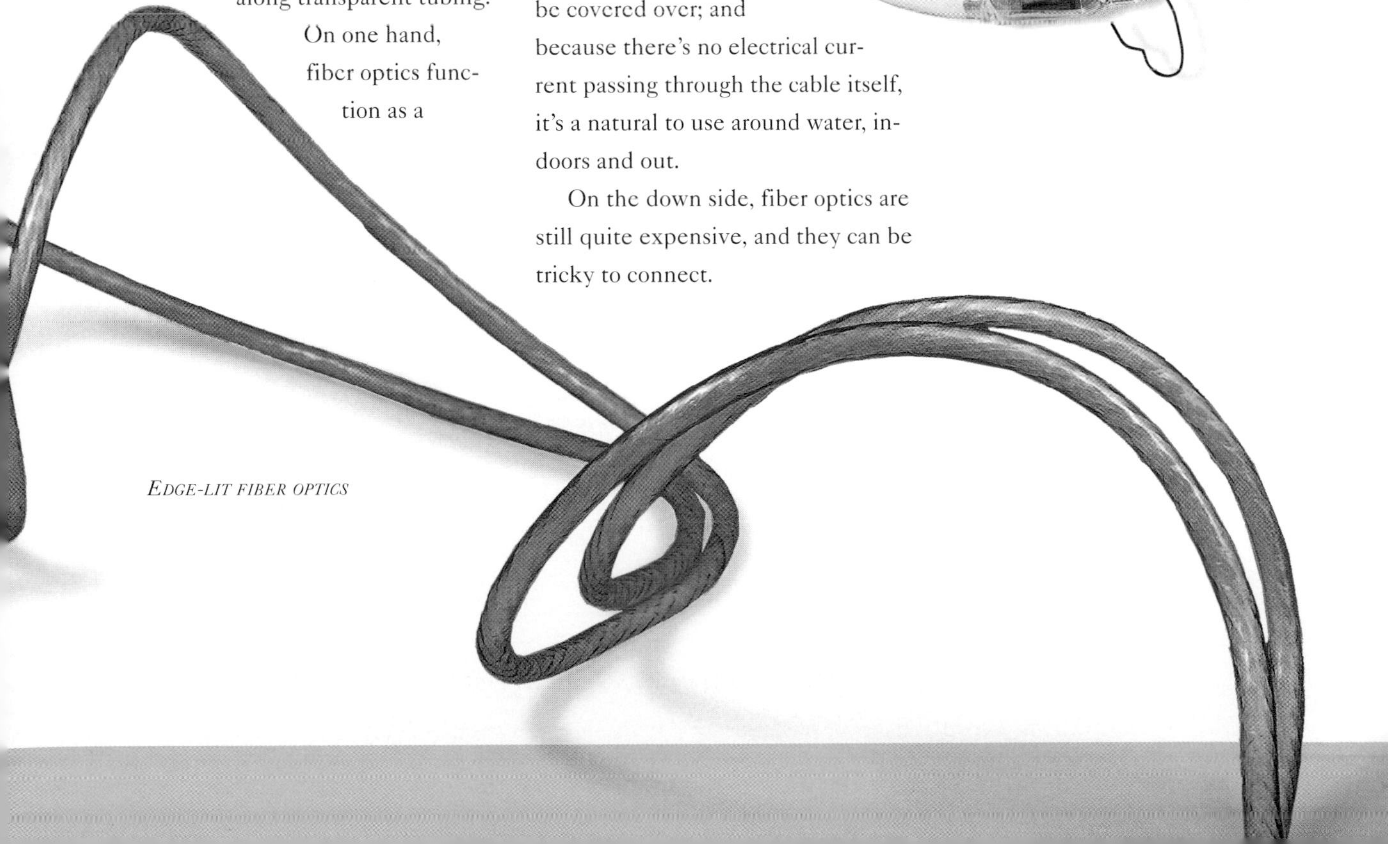

EDGE-LIT FIBER OPTICS

a shopper's guide

Bulb Comparisons at a Glance

		Description	Common Wattages	Efficiency (lumens per watt)
INCANDESCENT				
A-bulb		Familiar pear shape; frosted or clear.	15 to 250	13.5 to 18.5
Three-way		A-bulb shape; frosted; two filaments provide three light levels.	30/70/100 to 100/200/300	10 to 15
T—Tubular		Tube-shaped, from 5" long. Frosted or clear.	15 to 40	7.5 to 10
R—Reflector		White or silvered coating directs light out end of funnel-shaped bulb.	30 to 120	8 to 12.5
Silvered bowl		Same shape as A-bulb, with silvered cap to cut glare and produce indirect light.	25 to 60	8
G—Globe		Ball-shaped bulb, 2" to 6" in diameter; frosted or clear.	25 to 100	6 to 12
Flame-shaped (candle)		Decorative; specially coated; frosted or clear.	15 to 60	8 to 11
FLUORESCENT				
Tube		Tube-shaped, 5" to 96" long. Needs special fixture and ballast.	8 to 95	35 to 48
PL—Compact tube		U-shaped with base; 5¼" to 7½" long.	7 to 27	70 to 78
Circline		Circular, 6" to 16" in diameter; may replace A-bulbs or require special fixtures.	22 to 40	50 to 66
Compact bulb		Many shapes and sizes, replacing incandescent bulbs without needing special sockets.	11 to 42	41 to 58
QUARTZ HALOGEN				
Low-voltage MR-16 (mini-reflector)		Tiny (2" diameter) projector bulb; gives small circle of light from a distance.	20 to 75	14 to 19
PAR—Parabolic aluminized reflector		Similar to auto headlamps; special shape and coating project light and control beam.	50 to 120	8 to 13
Specialty		Small, clear bulb with consistently high light output; used in halogen fixtures only.	50 to 500	18 to 22
HIGH-INTENSITY DISCHARGE (HID)				
Mercury vapor		Bulb-within-a-bulb, shaped like an oversize A-bulb; needs special ballast.	100 to 250	63
Metal halide		Almost twice as efficient as old mercury vapor; needs special ballast and fixture.	175 to 400	71 to 100
High-pressure sodium		Orange-hued light; needs special ballast and fixture.	50 to 400	64 to 95

Color Temperature (K)	Bulb Life (hours)
2,800	750 to 2,500
2,800	1,000 to 1,600
2,800	1,000 to 1,500
2,800	1,000 to 2,000
2,700 to 3,000	1,000
2,800	1,500 to 2,500
2,800	1,500
2,700 to 6,300	7,500 to 20,000
2,700 to 6,300	9,000 to 10,000
2,700 to 4,200	12,000
2,700 to 6,300	9,000 to 10,000
2,925 to 3,050	2,000 to 4,000
3,050	2,000 to 6,000
3,050	2,000
3,300 to 3,900	16,000 to 24,000
3,700 to 4,000	7,500 to 20,000
2,100	16,000 to 24,000

High-intensity discharge (HID)

HID bulbs produce a lot of light while using a relatively small amount of power. You've seen them, but it's probably been in street lighting or public places. Requiring special fixtures and ballasts, these largish lights may take up to 7 minutes to ignite once switched on. The color emitted by most HID bulbs ranges from mildly to extremely unflattering; metal halide is a notable exception.

MERCURY VAPOR LIGHT is produced by a bulb-within-a-bulb shaped much like an oversize A-bulb. Fixtures are available for garden and security lighting. While color rendering is a ghoulish blue-green, it's usually acceptable for outdoor uses.

HIGH-PRESSURE SODIUM, a distinctively orangish source, is the number one choice for street lighting. It's also used indoors commercially and industrially. Like mercury vapor, high-pressure sodium bulbs require a special ballast and fixture.

LOW-PRESSURE SODIUM sports a U-shaped tube within a larger bulb. An even duller orange than its high-pressure counterpart, low-pressure sodium is even more efficient. Thus it's used extensively for highway and security lighting.

METAL HALIDE is the HID source most likely to come in from the cold in coming years. Why? Its color temperature is far more pleasant than most HIDs, ranging from 3,000°K to 4,000°K. The technology is similar to mercury vapor but almost twice as efficient.

In addition, metal halide bulbs can be made smaller than other HID sources, allowing for more attractive fixtures. While it's used primarily for outdoor security lighting, metal halide is now also available in table lamp wattages with integral ballasts.

MERCURY VAPOR   *METAL HALIDE*

HIGH-PRESSURE SODIUM

Movable Fixtures

EXPRESS YOURSELF

Table lamps, floor lamps, and small specialty lamps are easy to buy, easy to change, and easy to take along when you move. Within this category you'll find fixtures that will provide any quality of light you need. Be careful, though: while they can go a long way toward setting a design style, movable fixtures can look jumbled and busy if overused or mismatched. One solution is to think of them as either primarily decorative or task-specific and to use other, more discreet sources for ambient light.

TABLE LAMPS show individuality and style at the same time that they mark space or provide task light. Variety, mobility, and ease of installation add to their appeal. Styles range from quietly traditional to

TRADITIONAL TABLE LAMP

brashly avant-garde. Three-way and dimmable table lamps offer the most flexibility, letting you dial from an unobtrusive

background glow to bright task levels instantly.

The choice of a lampshade is crucial to the effectiveness of a table lamp. A difference of only 2 inches in the diameter of the shade's lower edge can make a significant difference in the spread of light. How opaque or translucent is the lampshade? Will it produce a warm, soft glow—or unwelcome glare?

The height of the bulb within a shade also affects the circle of illumination: light will spread farther when the bulb is set low in the shade. To adjust the shade height, you can use small extension screws on the lamp harp. Look for these screws at home centers and lighting supply stores.

FLOOR LAMPS offer great flexibility. A traditional floor lamp often provides a combination of light levels, serving either as a reading light or as a source of soft ambient light. Unobtrusive

MODERN TABLE LAMP

PHARMACY LAMP

TRADITIONAL FLOOR LAMP

TORCHÈRES

PAPER LAMP

TREE LAMP

pharmacy lamps, especially those with built-in dimmers, offer a range of options, particularly for tasks such as reading or sewing. Lamps with adjustable directional shades, such as two- or three-source lamps ("tree lamps"), are a practical choice for task lighting—but beware of glare.

TORCHÈRES—available in halogen, incandescent, and now compact fluorescent versions—bounce bright light onto the ceiling for a dramatic form of indirect lighting. However, the standard 8-foot ceiling often is too low for the typical 6- to 6½-foot-high torchère; in this case, look for one with a built-in diffuser to avoid creating a hot spot.

Some torchères include a dimmer unit for controlling light output. Fluorescent models tend to produce softer, more diffuse light than incandescent or halogen fixtures. They're energy-savers, too.

TASK LAMPS are sometimes just smaller, focused versions of traditional table lamps. *Adjustable-neck task lamps* supply a small, bright pool of light while leaving your immediate work area uncluttered. Halogen lamps produce the cleanest, tightest beam, while fluorescent models are tops for reducing glare and shadows. Some drafting lamps include both types of light, providing perhaps the best of both worlds. Easily adjusted *clip-on lights* are practical for providing task lighting over beds, desks, and shelves.

SPECIALTY LAMPS in new varieties are constantly appearing on the market. Some lamps—like the traditional picture light—can fill a specific need while remaining movable, and they require no special wiring.

Uplight cans highlight indoor plants or wash walls with light for instant decorating touches. *Aimable spotlights* are handy for pinpointing plants, paintings, or sculpture from nearby. *Picture lights* are inexpensive, easy-to-add options for accenting individual paintings or wall art. Available in several shapes and finishes, the lights simply screw to the back of the picture frame.

T-2 FLUORESCENT TASK LAMP

UPLIGHT CAN

CLIP-ON LIGHT

HALOGEN TASK LAMP

AIMABLE SPOTLIGHT

PICTURE LIGHT

*AIMABLE
TABLE LAMP*

NIGHT-LIGHTS, MOONLIGHTS

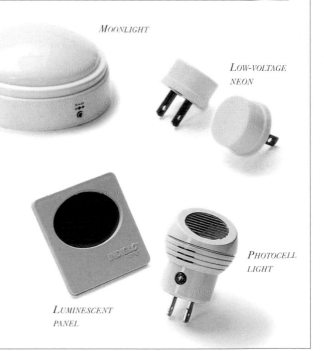

Plug-in night-lights consume only a few watts a night while scaring away bedroom goblins and aiding navigation through a darkened house. Neon plug-ins that glow in a variety of colors and electro-luminescent panels that gleam with a bluish or greenish tint use the merest trickle of electricity. Or you can opt for a pivoting plug-in light with a photocell— it turns on automatically at night and can be aimed along a hallway.

Then there are battery-operated lights, the ultimate movable fixture. A battery-powered "moonlight" turns on when you slap the globe, so there's no fumbling for a switch. Battery-driven fluorescent strips can supply handy, low-temperature light in closets and tight utility spaces where it's hard or awkward to run wires or find heat clearance for a standard fixture.

MOONLIGHT

*LOW-VOLTAGE
NEON*

*LUMINESCENT
PANEL*

*PHOTOCELL
LIGHT*

Surface-mounted Fixtures

FOR WALLS, CEILINGS, OR CABINETS

Installed on either walls or ceilings, surface-mounted fixtures are integral to most home lighting designs. They're especially good at providing diffuse ambient light, though some fixtures are highly decorative, too. Under-cabinet strips can supply effective task lighting in kitchens and workshops.

Most surface fixtures come with their own mounting hardware, adaptable to any standard fixture box. Heavier types—such as ceiling fan/light combinations or large chandeliers—may require beefier support, such as a mounting bar, hickey, or J-hook. Some pendants, wall sconces, and under-cabinet lights plug into a nearby receptacle.

FLUORESCENT CEILING GLOBE

AVANT-GARDE PENDANT

FLUSH-MOUNTED FIXTURES, which mount directly to a housing box, provide general illumination in traffic areas such as landings, entries, and hallways. Kitchens, bathrooms, and work-

shops often benefit from the added light of surface fixtures used in conjunction with task lighting on work surfaces.

Models in this category range from functional frosted glass globes to delicate, decorative wall fixtures. When considering a fixture, look closely at how light bounces off the wall or ceiling to make sure it will be directed where you want it.

Most traditional flush fixtures house incandescent A-bulbs, but new fluorescent globes with trim circline tubes (see page 97) are becoming more common.

When fluorescent panels sit against the ceiling, they're loosely named *shoplights;* when they're flush—as within a suspended ceiling—they're called *troffers.* The only real difference is that troffers aren't finished on the sides. Except in utility spaces, the tubes these fixtures house are usually covered with acrylic diffusing panels. Multiple panels may be grouped or "ganged," end-to-end or side-by-side, to make one large light source.

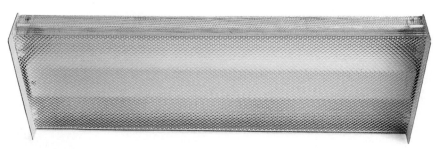

FLUORESCENT SHOPLIGHT

CEILING FAN/LIGHT

CHANDELIER

CHANDELIERS AND PENDANTS add sparkle and style in high-ceilinged entries and above dining tables and breakfast nooks. Depending on your needs, these decorative fixtures can give direct or diffused light—or a combination of the two. It's always a good idea to wire such fixtures to a dimmer, allowing you to fine-tune their output. Swags—chain-suspended pendants with cords and plugs—offer a movable alternative.

The size of a fixture relative to its surroundings is critical. A pendant used over a table should be at least 12 inches narrower than the table to keep diners or passersby from colliding with it. In an entry, be sure to allow enough room below a chandelier to guarantee safe passage for tall people.

WALL SCONCES, available in a huge array of styles, are great for hallways (providing they don't impede traffic) and for indirect lighting in living spaces. From the photos in the previous section, "Great Lighting Ideas," you can see that sconces often travel in pairs, flanking windows, doorways, fireplaces, or furniture groupings.

Place sconces about 5½ feet up from the floor, and keep them away from corners—otherwise, they'll create hot spots.

CEILING FAN/LIGHT COMBINATIONS can reduce your dependence on an air conditioner when the fan is used regularly. Or you can use one only as needed to improve the comfort of a room.

WALL SCONCES

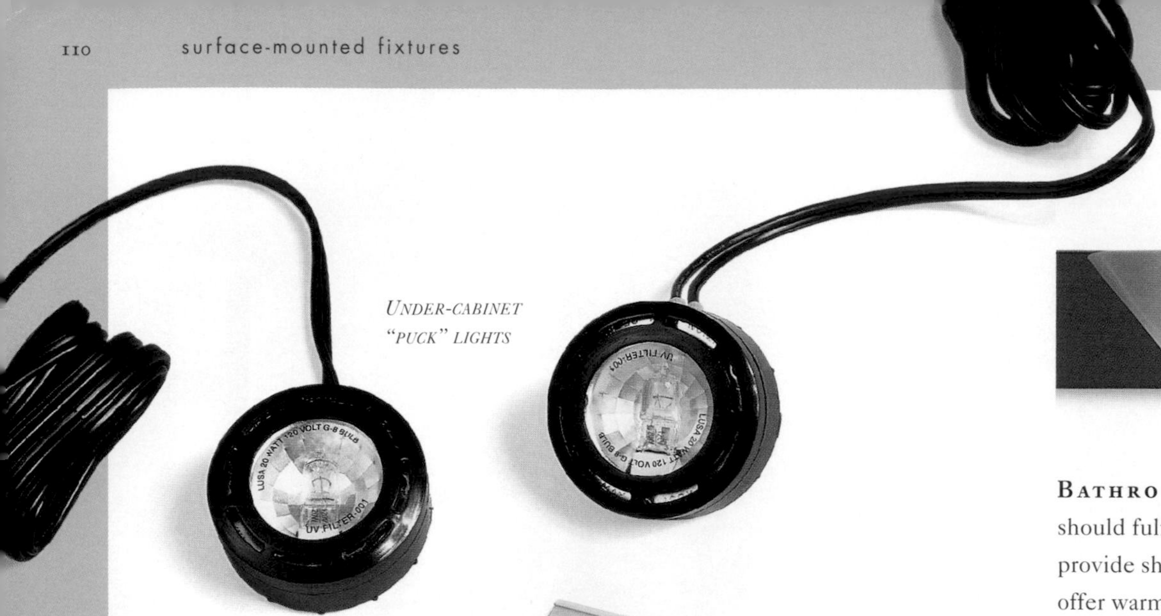

*UNDER-CABINET
"PUCK" LIGHTS*

BATHROOM MAKEUP LIGHTS
should fulfill two basic requirements:
provide shadow-free task lighting and
offer warm, smooth-toned color temperature. The classic choice is so-
called "theater lighting"—strings of

*UNDER-CABINET
FLUORESCENT LIGHT*

*HALOGEN
STRIP LIGHT*

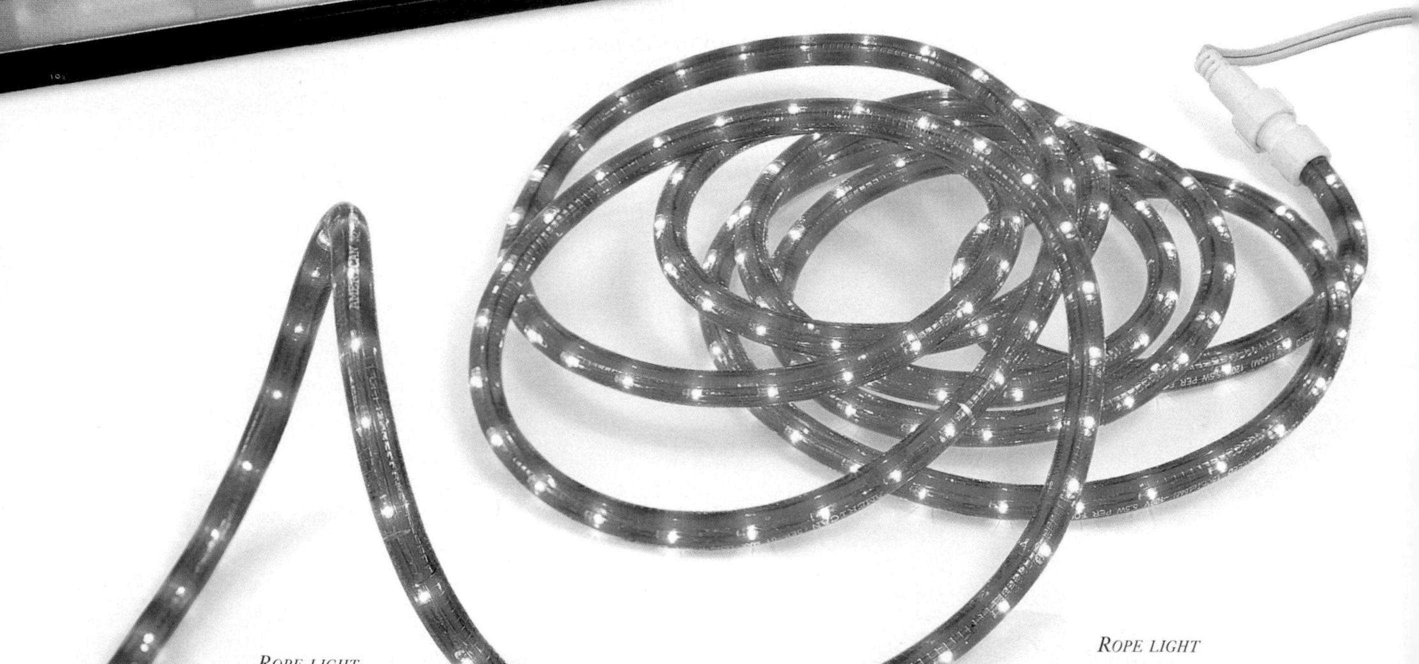

ROPE LIGHT

*ROPE LIGHT
CONNECTORS*

BATHROOM MAKEUP LIGHT

incandescent globes on a striplike base; you'll find several versions at most home centers. Other options abound, including vertically mounted fluorescent tubes, incandescent tubes (see page 95), and wall sconces flanking either side of a mirror.

UNDER-CABINET TASK LIGHTS come thin and narrow to fit the space below a kitchen's wall cabinets and shine on the countertop below. Fluorescents are popular here, in both plug-in and wire-in versions. These units, as thin as 1³⁄₁₆ inches, screw to the bottom of the cabinets. Lengths

from 12 inches on up are available; some can be "ganged" together to make longer runs.

Incandescent and halogen strips (see following) also make sense for under-cabinet use—particularly if you wish to be able to dim the lights.

STRIP LIGHTS are partly for fun, partly for effective task lighting. They add a splash of light and color to display niches, kitchen soffits, stair railings, architectural columns, or just about anywhere.

You'll find both rigid and flexible versions. Rigid strips, equipped with

tiny incandescent or halogen bulbs, are wired into a line with a semirigid metal or plastic backing; often they can be joined end-to-end to make longer strips. Fixtures with larger bulbs are also available; these are essentially miniature track systems (see pages 112–113).

Flexible versions called *rope lights* feature tiny bulbs encased in flexible plastic tubes. Rope lights are finding their way into home improvement centers, along with a full line of connectors to install them and splice runs into whatever shapes you choose.

MAKE YOUR MARK

Have you ever wanted to resurrect a favorite old fixture—or build your own from scratch? Prowl around most home improvement centers and you'll discover a sizable collection of table-lamp components: lamp harps, shades, cords, sockets, switches, bases—even complete kits containing all these pieces.

You'll also find a mix-and-match group of ceiling fixture parts and retrofits, such as canopies, globes, mounting hardware, even traditional plaster-of-paris escutcheons for chandeliers and ceiling fans.

Many lamp parts and kits come with assembly instructions. For details on fixture-wiring tools and techniques, see the Sunset book *Complete Home Wiring*.

SHADE

GLOBE

CANOPY

SOCKET

HARP

ESCUTCHEONS

CORD

Track Fixtures

EASY TO ADD, EASY TO AIM

Track lighting offers both versatility and ease of installation. Available in varying lengths, tracks are really electrical lines extended from the housing box they tie into (or the wall outlet they plug into); matching fixtures can be mounted anywhere along each line.

Early track fixtures were large and clunky, since they needed to house R (reflector) and PAR bulbs. Now they're becoming smaller and more stylish, especially those designed for low-voltage halogen bulbs. New cable lights (see facing page) are the latest development—even the "track" is getting smaller!

Tracks can accommodate pendant fixtures, clip-on lamps, and low-voltage spotlights as well as a large selection of standard spots. Some low-voltage fixtures have an integral transformer (which can sometimes be big and buzzy), while some fit a standard track by means of an adapter. Other tracks require an external transformer mounted away from the track (which can serve several tracks and lights). For details, see page 115.

For safety, avoid track lighting in damp areas such as bathrooms or laundry rooms.

MAKING CONNECTIONS. Standard track systems are mounted to the wall or ceiling either directly or with mounting clips. Power typically is provided by a wire-in saddle mounted to a housing box (plug-in units or adapters are also available). A "floating" saddle lets you tie in anywhere along the track, not just at one end.

Track connectors make it possible to extend some systems indefinitely—in a straight line, at an angle, or even in a rectangular pattern. Most systems offer a host of connector options.

Tracks come in one- and multi-circuit varieties; the multi-circuit type allows you to operate two or more sets of lights independently.

ACCESSORIES. You can modify light output or direct it away from people's sight lines with track fixture accessories. Lenses

PLUG-IN ADAPTERS

FLEXIBLE CONNECTORS

120-VOLT FIXTURE

LOW-VOLTAGE FIXTURE WITH INTEGRAL TRANSFORMER

TRACK CONNECTORS

TRACK PENDANT

focus or diffuse light, louvers cut glare, and baffles and barndoors cut or shape light output. Filters can add subtle or not-so-subtle color accents.

CABLE LIGHTS. After illuminating shops and showrooms for years, these low-voltage lights are now gaining popularity with homeowners. Minimalist, futuristic, fantastic, or whimsical, the diminutive fixtures are designed to be at once notable and discreet.

A cable light system has four basic components: power source, cables, lights, and mounting hardware. Some manufacturers offer basic kits that can be installed by homeowners; more elaborate systems may require professional installation.

At the heart of each fixture is the exposed light: a tiny halogen MR-11 or MR-16 bulb (see page 98). Transformers can simply be plugged into a wall outlet or wired into a ceiling box, in some cases, or be located remotely, with wires run to the room. The cables run in parallel pairs spaced

from 1 inch to more than 6 inches apart, depending on the fixtures used. Support brackets, cable anchors, and turnbuckles complete the picture; how much of this hardware you need depends on the complexity of your installation.

CABLE LIGHT KIT

LOW-VOLTAGE FIXTURE AND CABLE

Recessed Fixtures

MIX AND MATCH

Recessed downlights offer effective light without the intrusion of a visible fixture. Basically domes with light bulbs set into their tops, most fixtures can be fitted with any of a number of bulb types and sizes, trims, and accessories that shape the light to the desired function. When installed, only the trim is visible, not the fixture itself.

Low-voltage downlights—particularly those with MR-16 bulbs—are especially popular for tight accent lighting. For a longer throw or more impact, choose low- or standard-voltage PAR bulbs in aimable fixture housings rather than MR-16s. Like their track counterparts, many low-voltage

NEW-WORK HOUSING

CUT-IN HOUSING

downlights include an integral transformer; or you can use a single remote transformer (see facing page) to serve a number of fixtures.

Downlights make good ambient sources, too, and some can now be fitted with energy-saving fluorescent bulbs (see pages 96–97). However, designers have learned not to trust downlights for task lighting—one's head tends to block the light from the task at hand!

START WITH THE HOUSING. Downlights are usually prewired and grounded to their own junction boxes. These fixtures need several inches of clearance above the ceiling, so they're most easily installed below an unfin-

ished attic or crawl space. If space is tight, you can purchase low-clearance fixtures.

So-called "new-work" units, used in new construction, are easy to secure between exposed ceiling members. Cut-in or remodeling models are also available—they slip into, then clip onto, a hole cut in the existing ceiling.

Many downlights produce a lot of heat, so you must either remove insulation within 3 inches of the fixture or buy an "IC" fixture rated for direct contact with surrounding materials.

CHOOSE THE TRIM. Trim rings, baffles, lenses, and louvers are modular accessories in most downlight lines: pick the one you want and snap it in place. Besides shaping the light, the

SLOT APERTURE

AIMABLE APERTURE

trim ring covers the rough edges of the fixture housing and ceiling hole, providing an attractive integral look.

A sampling of trim rings and other accessories is shown on this page. Brass and chrome reflector rings bounce extra light; black baffles cut it off. Slot apertures shape tight accent patterns; aimable eyeballs allow wider patterns. Acrylic lenses soften light and cut glare, as do honeycomb louvers.

LOW-VOLTAGE LOGISTICS

Smaller, safer, and more energy-efficient than standard 120-volt systems, low-voltage light fixtures have become popular indoors as well as out. Low-voltage lights use a transformer to step down household current to 12 or 24 volts; you can buy prepackaged systems or create your own with individual fixtures.

Low-voltage tracks or downlights may include an integral transformer, or you can use a remote external transformer to serve a number of fixtures. Both options are shown.

Which arrangement is best? Both have pluses and minuses. Integral transformers are convenient, especially when only one or two fixtures are involved. But the built-in unit makes the fixture bulkier and more expensive; some integral units may also hum, especially when coupled with dimmers. A remote transformer housed in a nearby closet, basement, or ceiling can serve

INTEGRAL TRANSFORMER

EXTERNAL TRANSFORMER

a number of fixtures; but you will have to hassle with more routing and calculate what wire size you'll need. The size of the transformer limits the total wattage of lamps that can be hooked up to it.

TRIM RINGS

Controls

TURN IT ON—BY HAND OR COMPUTER

Switches, timers, and dimmers—collectively called controls—provide the key to fine-tuning a layered, flexible lighting scheme.

Besides the classic two-way toggle, you'll also find three- and four-way switches, pilot switches, motion sensors, timers, and a wide range of dimmer designs (see page 118). New offerings appear constantly.

Standard switches

The classic single-pole switch controls a light or an outlet from one location only. It comes in 15- and 20-amp models—pick the switch that matches your circuit rating. Modern versions include a grounding connection; older switches have two hot terminals only.

Three-way switches operate in pairs to control lights or receptacles from two locations—such as the opposite ends of a hallway. Four-way switches are used only in combination with three-way switches to control lights or receptacles from more than two locations.

A pilot switch has a toggle that glows when the fixture is on. Pilot switches often are used for lights that may be out of sight and mind—as in the basement, the attic, or outdoors.

Basic switches often come in several grades: the cheapest grade is "residential" or "contractor"; higher-quality models are called "heavy-duty," "commercial," or "spec." "Designer" switches may

be so named for their looks only, not for the grade of construction.

Unlike the lowly plug-in receptacle, switches are now available in a wide range of colors, finishes, and toggle designs—even night-light versions that glow in the dark.

Receptacles

What if your fixture has a plug? For walls, choose a standard duplex (two-outlet) receptacle or—in potentially wet areas—a shockproof GFCI (ground fault circuit interrupter). Depending on how it's wired, the standard receptacle may have both of its outlets "hot," both outlets switch-controlled, or one outlet hot and the other switch-controlled. This last option is handy in living rooms and bedrooms where movable lamps and other electronics mingle.

THREE-WAY SWITCH

FOUR-WAY SWITCH

PILOT SWITCH

SINGLE-POLE DESIGNER SWITCH

FLOOR OUTLET

MOTION-SENSOR SWITCH

And what if your floor plan calls for furniture groupings—and attendant lamps—in the center of the room? Enter the floor outlet. A well-placed floor outlet keeps lamp cords out of sight and out of harm's way.

Motion-sensor switches

Used for security, convenience, or energy savings, a motion-sensor switch turns on a light (or lights) when it detects movement in a room, then shuts it off after a predetermined interval. Both single-pole and three-way versions are available. Better designs allow you to adjust for sensitivity and time interval and include a manual ON/OFF lever.

For motion sensors used in outdoor lighting, see page 124.

Timers

Timers come in wire-in and plug-in versions. The former replaces a standard wall switch; the latter plugs into a receptacle, and movable lamps are then plugged into the timer.

Standard wire-in timer switches allow you to set a light or other device to turn on at preset time intervals. Programmable timer switches take things one step further, providing multiple daily settings or even weekly cycles for security lights, a fan, even the television. If a fixture is controlled by two different switches, purchase a three-way timer; otherwise, buy a single-pole timer.

Unlike most other switches, some timer switches require a neutral wire as well as the hot wires—so you may need to wire these in from scratch rather than simply replacing your existing switches.

A plug-in timer can turn a lamp on several times a day and for several days in a row, depending on how fancy the version is and where you position the tabs around the dial.

PLUG-IN TIMER

WIRE-IN TIMER SWITCH

PROGRAMMABLE TIMER SWITCH

Dimmer switches

Originally called rheostats, dimmers take the place of standard switches in wall-mounted housing boxes. When dialed down, a dimmer essentially "clips off" part of the electrical current flowing to the light. Numerous styles are available, some with presets and fade controls.

Get a dimmer that matches your voltage and the bulb type. Standard-voltage incandescents and halogens

PRESET DIMMER SWITCHES

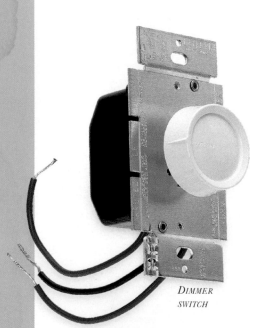

DIMMER SWITCH

are relatively easy to dim. You'll want a low-voltage dimmer for low-voltage lights. To minimize humming or potential interference (as from radio or television), match the dimmer type to the low-voltage transformer in use—either magnetic (older) or solid-state (better).

Dimmers are rated for maximum wattage. For line-voltage models, 600 watts is the standard; you can also find 1,000-watt versions. Some low-voltage dimmers may handle only 300 watts.

Fluorescent lights require fluorescent dimmers and, just as important, a dimming ballast in the fixture itself. This can be a problematic retrofit—it may be easier to simply replace an existing fixture with one that's dimmable. Solid-state dimmers and ballasts work best.

If you have a three-way setup—a light controlled by two switches that do not have ON and OFF printed on their toggles—only one of the switches can be a dimmer. Replace the three-way switch most often used with a three-way dimmer, and leave the second three-way switch in place. For a fixture controlled by a single switch, purchase a single-pole dimmer.

In-line dimmers

A number of devices can be used to convert an ordinary lamp into one that dims. You can plug a table lamp or a floor lamp into a dimmer that in turn plugs into a wall outlet. Or you can screw a light bulb into a lamp-base

dimmer, then screw the assembly into a lamp's light bulb socket. With a little more work, you can add an in-line dimmer to a lamp cord. All three devices are shown below.

IN-LINE DIMMERS

Control panels

More controls mean extra clutter from ganged switches and dimmers. New multiscene control panels do away with all this and allow you to quickly dial in a preset number of lighting "scenes." Panels controlling six or so scenes can fit into a standard housing box; larger panels require a special box and more involved wiring.

Look for control panels that have gentle fades between scenes and manual ON/OFF overrides. A panel with a "panic button" lets you dial every light to full strength instantly.

Centralized control systems—those that consolidate the lights for an entire house—require a dedicated closet or crawl space area. Increasingly, these sophisticated systems are controlled by a computer with the potential to link indoor lights to a household alarm system, outdoor security lighting, audio visual wiring, and telecommunications. The "smart house" is here—for a price, of course.

Wiring integrated systems can be quite involved, so they're difficult to retrofit in existing spaces. But if you're building or remodeling, many experts recommend that you install a wiring "chase" and run Cat-5 communications cable, coaxial cable, A/V wires, and even fiber optics from room to room, awaiting future technologies.

CAT-5 CABLE

GOING WIRELESS

New technology might be a lot easier to install if it weren't for all those wires! In fact, radio-controlled switches and dimmers that can control a lamp, a chandelier, or a ceiling fan/light combination are widely available. These push-button transmitters have ON/OFF and dimming capabilities. Besides the handheld remote, you need just a small receiver unit, which usually tucks into an existing fixture canopy or housing box. You'll need to wire the receiver to the fixture.

More ambitious "X-10" technology includes not only keychain button transmitters but larger keypads that control up to 16 lights. The transmitter powers a receiver on each fixture, light socket, dimmer, or wall outlet. How well do these systems work? The jury is still out.

FAN/LIGHT REMOTE

RECEIVER

X-10 REMOTE SYSTEM

CONTROL PANEL

Outdoor Lighting

MAKE IT SUBTLE, BRIGHT, OR BOTH

What's your preference: line-voltage fixtures, low-voltage fixtures, or both? A 120-volt outdoor lighting system offers several advantages over a 12-volt system (see pages 122–123)—especially when security, not aesthetics, is the issue. For starters, 120-volt fixtures usually illuminate larger areas than 12-volt fixtures can—useful both for security and for lighting trees from the ground. The bigger fixtures are also sturdier, and their buried cables and connections provide a look of permanence lacking in some low-voltage systems.

On the other hand, 12-volt systems are simpler to install—especially for homeowners. And the cable and smaller fixtures can snake just about anywhere you need them.

Confused? It helps to choose the bulbs you want first (see pages 94–103) and then the appropriate fixtures. For instance, low-voltage halogen MR-16 bulbs are popular for accenting; PAR spots and floods, available in both standard and low voltage, are best for lighting trees or wide areas.

120-volt systems

A 120-volt outdoor system consists of a set of light fixtures and either type UF (underground feeder) cable, if allowed by local code, or individual wires run inside rigid metal or PVC conduit. (All three materials are shown on the facing page.)

Keep in mind that 120-volt wire splices and fixture connections must always occur inside a housing box. Boxes for exterior use come in two types: so-called driptight boxes that deflect vertically falling water and watertight boxes that keep out water coming from any direction. For any-place likely to get wet, a watertight box is best. All covers for watertight boxes are sealed with gaskets. The outdoor fixture box shown on the facing page is typical.

FLUORESCENT FLOODLIGHT

POST LIGHT

PATH LIGHT

RIGID
METAL CONDUIT

PVC
CONDUIT

UF CABLE

OUTDOOR FIXTURE BOX

OUTDOOR
DOWNLIGHT

Fixtures for 120-volt outdoor systems range from well lights and other portable uplights to post lights that mark front walks, spread lights that illuminate paths or bridges, and downlights designed to be anchored to the house wall, eaves, or trees.

Outdoor fixtures come in various sizes, mostly made of bronze, cast or extruded aluminum, copper, or plastic. But you can also find decorative fixtures in stone, concrete, porcelain, and wood (redwood, cedar, and teak weather best). When evaluating fixtures, look for gaskets, high-quality components at joints and pivot points, and locking devices for aiming the fixtures.

SUBMERSIBLE
POOL LIGHT

WELL LIGHT

COLORED FILTERS

Low-voltage systems

Although low-voltage fixtures lack the punch of standard-current fixtures, their output is sufficient for most outdoor applications. Since it carries only 12 volts, low-voltage wiring doesn't present the dangers of 120 volts, nor does it require the special conduit and boxes of other outdoor wiring. All you need is a plug-in transformer, 12-volt cable, and low-voltage fixtures. To make things even easier, you'll find kits containing all these components at home and garden centers.

NUTS AND BOLTS. The transformer, usually housed in an integral driptight box, steps down 120-volt household current to 12 volts. Plug it into a nearby receptacle, then run the 12-volt cable from the low-voltage side of the transformer to where you want your lights. The cable can be buried a few inches deep or simply covered with mulch in a planting area; but to avoid accidentally spading through it, consider running the cable alongside structures, walks, and fences where you won't be likely to cultivate.

LOW-VOLTAGE TRANSFORMER

WEATHERPROOF OUTLET COVER

Some low-voltage light fixtures clip right onto the wire, while others require a clamp connector and still others must be spliced into the system and connected with wire nuts. Be sure to use the wire and connections specified in the instructions. If you don't already have a receptacle to plug the transformer into, install a GFCI-protected outlet and weatherproof cover (shown above).

SIZING YOUR SYSTEM. Most 12-volt transformers are rated for loads of 100 to 300 watts. In most cases, you simply add up the wattages of all the fixtures you wish to install, then choose a transformer and cable size that can handle the load.

PORTABLE "ROCK" LIGHTS

MOVABLE UPLIGHT

*OUTDOOR
STEP LIGHTS*

For long cable runs, however, you
must "de-rate" the circuit to account
for "voltage drop"—the accumulated
resistance in all that wire. The
solution? Drop a fixture or
two or beef up the cable
size. Your kit or cable will
probably come with
guidelines.

*OUTDOOR
PARTY LIGHTS*

*LOW-VOLTAGE
LIGHT AND CABLE*

*LOW-VOLTAGE
BOLLARD LIGHT*

Outdoor Controls

THESE DEVICES DO ALL THE WORK

How can you set up landscape or security lights to take care of themselves? A timer is one solution. Two other options are daylight-sensitive photocells and motion-sensor fixtures or add-ons.

DAYLIGHT SENSORS. These are simply photocells that react to daylight. When it's dark, the photocell sends power to the light fixture it's connected to; come dawn, the sensor opens the circuit, shutting down the fixture. You can install fixtures with built-in photocells or buy sensors separately.

Several retrofits are shown on the facing page. The most common type is a large photocell mounted directly onto a knockout in an outdoor fixture box. You can also buy a simple screw-base adapter with built-in sensor that fits a standard bulb socket; the bulb screws into the adapter. Or opt for a

MOTION-SENSOR FIXTURE

discreet photo eye designed to fit a hole drilled in a lamppost.

MOTION SENSORS. Handy both for security and for unloading a batch of groceries after dark, these "remote eyes" come in two basic versions:

MOTION-SENSOR ADD-ONS

infrared and microwave. Some units combine both wave types. Like daylight sensors, motion sensors can be purchased alone or integrated into a fixture that houses one or more floodlights (as shown at left and above).

Plan to install the motion sensor on a house wall, eaves, or a freestanding post, no higher than about 12 feet off the ground. The trick is aiming the sensor's detection lobes or waves. Don't align them so they're parallel to the most likely traffic path (for example, a front walkway); there are "dead spots" between the parallel detection bands. Instead, place the sensor so the lobes will cut across the traffic area.

Some motion sensors have adjustable ranges of sensitivity and can be set to remain on for varying lengths of time. Achieving just the right combination of aim, response level, and duration will probably take some trial and error.

TIMERS. If your outdoor lighting circuit begins indoors, you can control it with the same switches and timers shown on pages 116–117. But if your system connects outdoors, choose one of the hardier outdoor timers shown at right.

There's nothing fancy about the gunmetal gray timer shown at far right—it turns lights and other electrical devices on and off once a day. But it can handle heavy loads (up to 4,100 watts); it has a rugged, driptight hous-

DIGITAL SENSOR/TIMER

HEAVY-DUTY OUTDOOR TIMER

SECURITY LIGHT WITH BUILT-IN PHOTOCELL

DAYLIGHT SENSORS

ing that withstands abuse; and you can lock the cover.

If you have a string of plug-in outdoor lights (such as Christmas lights, decorative patio lights, or rope lights), attach the digital sensor/timer combo shown above left to the side of your house, plug it into an outlet, and then plug the lights into the unit. You can control the lights with the daylight sensor, the timer, or the manual ON/OFF switch.

HARNESS THE SUN

Costing nothing at all to operate, solar-powered garden lights collect all the energy they need from the sun by means of solar cells mounted atop each light. Such fixtures, though not exceptionally bright, can adequately mark a pathway or decorate a planting bed.

Just stick the stake-mounted lights into the ground and wait. It may take them a few days to achieve full strength, but when they do they'll go on automatically when darkness falls and recharge again during the daylight hours.

SOLAR FIXTURES

design and photography credits

design

FRONT MATTER

1 Architect: Remick Associates Architects-Builders, Inc.; Interior designer: Donna White Interiors **2** Product supplier: The Gardener **4** Lighting designer: Catherine Ng/Lightsmiths Design Group; Architect: Steve MacCracken **5** Lighting designer: Catherine Ng/Lightsmiths Design Group; Architect: The Bradley Group; Designer: Eckhard Evers

A PLANNING PRIMER

6 Lighting designer: Linda Ferry; Architect: Charles Rose; General contractor: Dennis Jones **8** Interior design: Jennifer Bevans Interiors **9 top left** Lighting designer: Catherine Ng/Lightsmiths Design Group; Architect/engineer: Roger Hartley; Interior architecture and design: Jessica Hall Associates; Interior finishes: Melinda Field Carwile/Field Studio **9 center** Design: Brian A. Murphy and Fro Vakili, BAM Construction/Design **9 bottom** Lighting designer: Catherine Ng/Lightsmiths Design Group; Architect/engineer: Roger Hartley; Interior architecture and design: Jessica Hall Associates; Interior finishes: Melinda Field Carwile/Field Studio **10–11** Lighting designer: Randall Whitehead Lighting Inc.; Architect: Erikson Zebroski Design Group **20 top right** LIMN **21 left** Architect: Remick Associates Architects-Builders, Inc.; Interior designer: Gary Hutton Designs **23** Lighting design and installa-tion: Berghoff Design Group; Technical support: Jonathan Hille

GREAT LIGHTING IDEAS

26 Designer: John Malick and Associates **28** Interior design: McWhorter/Ross Design Group **29** Lighting designer: Catherine Ng/Lightsmiths Design Group; Architect/engineer: Roger Hartley; Interior architecture and design: Jessica Hall Associates; Interior finishes: Melinda Field Carwile/Field Studio **30 top** Lighting designer: Catherine Ng/Lightsmiths Design Group; Architect: Steve MacCracken; Interior designer: Ron Smith **30 bottom** Lighting designer: Randall Whitehead Lighting Inc.; Architect: Erikson Zebroski Design Group **31** Light-ing designer: Linda Ferry; Archi-tect: Charles Rose; General contractor: Dennis Jones **32** Lighting designer: Catherine Ng/Lightsmiths Design Group; Interior designer: Judith Owen Interiors; Custom home builder: The Owen Companies **33** Interior designer: Marilyn Riding; Neon artist: Brian Coleman/Tercera Gallery **34 left** Design: Idea House at San Francisco Design Center **34–35** Lighting designer: Linda Ferry; Architect: Lee Von Hasseln **36** Lighting designer: Catherine Ng/Lightsmiths Design Group; Interior designer: Barbara Jacobs Interior Design **37 top** Lighting designer: Randall Whitehead Lighting Inc.; Architect: Erikson Zebroski Design Group **37 bottom** Architect: Brian Murphy **38** Lighting designer: Linda Ferry; Design: Pat & Bob Grace **39 top** Interior design: Richard Witzel & Associates **39 bottom** Product supplier: The Gardener **40** Lighting design-er: Bryan Burkhart/California Architectural Lighting **41 bottom** Design: Brian A. Murphy and Fro Vakili/BAM Construction/ Design **42** Lighting designer: Linda Ferry; Architect: Charles Rose; General contractor: Dennis Jones **43 bottom** Interior design: Sanborn Design, Inc. and Courtyard Collections **44** Lighting designer: Becca Foster Lighting Design; Architect: Michael Harris Architecture; Contractor: Pete Moffat Construction **45** Lighting designer: Melinda Morrison; Architect: Kuth/Ranieri **46** Light-ing designer: Linda Ferry; Design: Pat & Bob Grace **48 top** Light-ing designer: Linda Ferry; Interior designer: Alissa Lillie/Marie Fisher Interiors; Architect: Brian Peters; Cabinet design: Sheron Bailey Curutchet **48 bottom** Lighting designer: Bryan Burkhart/ California Architectural Lighting **49** Design: Josh Schweitzer/ Schweitzer BIM **50** Lighting designer: Linda Ferry; Architect: Charles Rose; Interior designer: Michelle Pheasant Design **51 top** Lighting designer: Epifanio Juarez/Juarez Design; Architect: Marc Randall Robinson; Interior architecture and design: Scott Design **51 bottom** Interior designer: Eugenia Erskine Esberg/ EJ Interior Design **52** Lighting designer: Linda Ferry; Architect: Eric Miller Architects, Inc.; Glass artist: Ahnalisa Miller **53** Architect: Marc Randall Robinson; Lighting designer: Epifanio Juarez/Juarez Design; Interior architecture and design: Scott Design **54** Architect: Backen, Arragoni & Ross **55 top** Architect: James Gillam Architects; Design: Jan Nissen Laidley **55 bottom** Lighting designer: Linda Ferry; Interior designer: Edward Perrault Design Associates, Inc. **56 top and bottom** Lighting designer: Linda Ferry; Architect: Eric Miller Architects, Inc.; Candle ring and sconce: Carl Olsen **56–57** Lighting designer: Catherine Ng/Lightsmiths Design Group; Architect: Steve MacCracken; Interior designer: Ron Smith **58** Architect: Kuth/Ranieri Architects **59** Lighting designer: Terry Ohm; Interior designer: Ann Maurice Interior Design **60** Design: Nick Cann/Graphics + Design **61 top** Lighting design-er: Epifanio Juarez/Juarez Design **61 bottom** Lighting designer: Becca Foster Lighting Design; Architect: Michael Harris Architecture; Contractor: Pete Moffat Construction **62** Lighting designer: Linda Ferry; Architect: Lee Von Hasseln **63** Lighting designer: Linda Ferry; Architect: Brian Peters; Interior designer: Alissa Lillie/Marie Fisher Interiors; Cabinet design: Sheron Bailey Curutchet **64** Lighting designer: Linda Ferry; Architect: Charles Rose; General contractor: Dennis Jones **65 bottom** Interior and lighting design: Kenton Knapp **66** Architect: Kuth/Ranieri Archi-tects **67 top** Lighting designer: Becca Foster Lighting Design; Architect: Michael Harris Architec-ture; Contractor: Pete Moffat Construction **67 bottom** Lighting designer: Randall Whitehead Lighting Inc.; Architect: Erikson

A SHOPPER'S GUIDE

BACK MATTER

photography

index

Numbers in **boldface type** refer to photographs.